- INSTALL ELECTRICAL BREAKERS FOR ENTIRE SHOP WITHIN EASY REACH, CIRCUIT-RATED FOR SUFFICIENT AMPERAGE

- STOCK FIRST AID KIT WITH MATERIALS TO TREAT CUTS, GASHES, SPLINTERS, FOREIGN OBJECTS AND CHEMICALS IN EYES, AND BURNS

- HAVE TELEPHONE IN SHOP TO CALL FOR HELP

- INSTALL FIRE EXTINGUISHER RATED FOR A-, B-, AND C-CLASS FIRES

- WEAR EYE PROTECTION AT ALL TIMES

- LOCK CABINETS AND POWER TOOLS TO PROTECT CHILDREN AND INEXPERIENCED VISITORS

- USE DUST COLLECTOR TO KEEP SHOP DUST AT A MINIMUM

- WEAR SHIRT SLEEVES ABOVE ELBOWS

- WEAR CLOSE-FITTING CLOTHES

- WEAR LONG PANTS

- REMOVE WATCHES, RINGS, OR JEWELRY

- KEEP TABLE AND FENCE SURFACES WAXED AND RUST-FREE

- WEAR THICK-SOLED SHOES, PREFERABLY WITH STEEL TOES

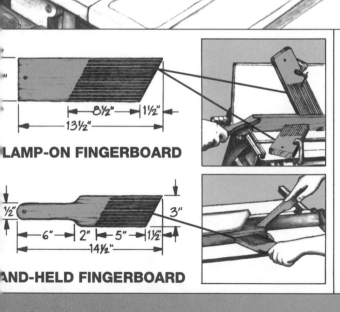

LAMP-ON FINGERBOARD

├─ 8½" ─┤─ 1½" ─┤
├──── 13½" ────┤

½"

├─ 6" ─┤ 2" ┤─ 5" ─┤ 1½"
├────── 14½" ──────┤

3"

AND-HELD FINGERBOARD

PROTECTION

WEAR FULL FACE SHIELD DURING LATHE TURNING, ROUTING, AND OTHER OPERATIONS THAT MAY THROW CHIPS

WEAR DUST MASK DURING SANDING AND SAWING

WEAR VAPOR MASK DURING FINISHING

WEAR SAFETY GLASSES OR GOGGLES AT ALL TIMES

WEAR RUBBER GLOVES FOR HANDLING DANGEROUS CHEMICALS

WEAR EAR PROTECTORS DURING ROUTING, PLANING, AND LONG, CONTINUOUS POWER TOOL OPERATION

THE WORKSHOP COMPANION®

FINISH CARPENTRY

TECHNIQUES FOR BETTER WOODWORKING

by Nick Engler

Rodale Press
Emmaus, Pennsylvania

Printed in the United States of America on acid-free ∞, recycled ♲ paper

If you have any questions or comments concerning this book, please write:
  Rodale Press
  Book Readers' Service
  33 East Minor Street
  Emmaus, PA 18098

About the Author: Nick Engler is an experienced woodworker, writer, and teacher. He worked as a luthier for many years, making traditional American musical instruments before he founded *Hands On!* magazine. Today, he contributes to several woodworking magazines and teaches woodworking at the University of Cincinnati. He has written more than 35 books.

Series Editor: Kevin Ireland
Editors: Bob Moran
        Roger Yepsen
Copy Editor: Sarah Dunn
Graphic Designer: Linda Watts
Illustrator: Mary Jane Favorite
Master Craftsman: Jim McCann
Photographer: Karen Callahan
Cover Photographer: Mitch Mandel
Proofreader: Hue Park
Indexer: Beverly Bremer
Typesetting by Computer Typography, Huber Heights, Ohio
Interior and endpaper illustrations by Mary Jane Favorite
Produced by Bookworks, Inc., West Milton, Ohio

Library of Congress Cataloging-in-Publication Data

Engler, Nick.
    Finish carpentry/by Nick Engler.
        p.   cm. — (The workshop companion)
    Includes index.
    ISBN 0–87596–583–0   hardcover
    1. Finish carpentry.   I. Title   II. Series:
Engler, Nick.   Workshop companion.
TH5640.E53   1994
694'.6—dc20   94–22277
                                     CIP

2 4 6 8 10 9 7 5 3   hardcover

Special Thanks to:

Paul Miller
American Marketing and Distributing
  Company
Cincinnati, Ohio

Balsbaugh Builders, Inc.
Englewood, Ohio

Larry Callahan
West Milton, Ohio

Dayton Door Sales
Dayton, Ohio

Eagle Windows and Doors
Dubuque, Iowa

Georgia-Pacific Corporation
Atlanta, Georgia

Hyde Park Lumber Company
Cincinnati, Ohio

Wertz Hardware
West Milton, Ohio

CONTENTS

TECHNIQUES

PROJECTS

TECHNIQUES

1

FINISHING YOUR HOME: A CONTINUING PROJECT

Finish carpentry is the woodworking you must do to finish a house *after* the structure is built. It includes nonstructural elements such as windows, doors, wood floor and wall coverings, moldings, railings, and other trim work — all the touches that give a house a finished appearance. It requires a knowledge of carpentry and fine woodworking, yet remains a craft all its own.

For those among us who finish our own houses, finish carpentry is a pursuit that begins the moment we move in and ends when we leave. We're constantly adding or changing details to refine the appearance of the building and make it our own. In short, finish carpentry is what craftsmen do to make a house a home.

HOW A HOUSE IS FINISHED

THE ANATOMY OF A HOUSE

Before you begin a finish carpentry project, it's best to know what sort of framing is behind those walls. The vast majority of homes in the United States are *stick-built*. They have a wooden frame nailed together from *"two-by" lumber* (2x4s, 2x6s, and so on) and this framework is covered with various materials.

Framework — There are two types of building frames. In a *platform frame,* the floors, walls, and roof are built one on top of the other, from the ground up. Most contemporary homes are framed this way. Many older homes, however, have a *balloon frame.* The walls and roof are built first, then the floors are suspended from the walls. *(SEE FIGURE 1-1.)*

Walls — The walls of most homes are framed with vertical members or *studs* spaced 16 to 24 inches apart, then covered. The inside walls of older homes

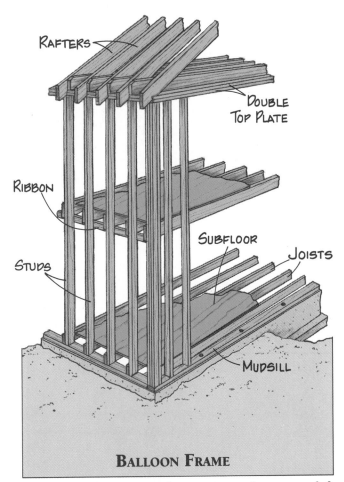

BALLOON FRAME

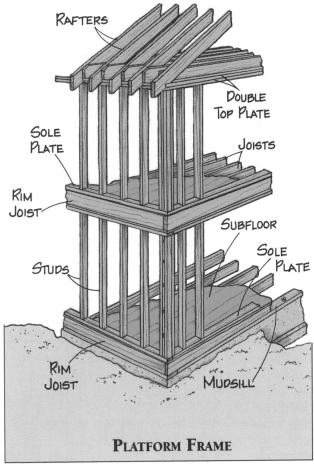

PLATFORM FRAME

1-1 Although some North American homes are built of masonry or framed with heavy timbers, most are *stick-built* — framed with two-by lumber and sheathed in any one of several ways. Old houses often have a *balloon frame,* as shown on the left. The vertical wall studs extend from the foundation to the roof and the floors are suspended from them. Roughly a century ago, however, primary growth forests were depleted and it became more difficult to obtain the long lumber needed for balloon framing. Carpenters began to construct **platform frames,** as shown on the right. In a platform frame, each floor is a platform that supports the framing members above it. The wall studs only stretch the height of a single story.

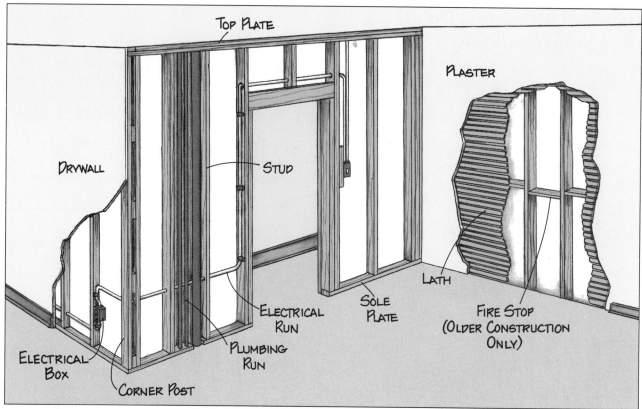

1-2 The walls in most homes are framed with two-by lumber and covered with various materials. Those in older homes are often covered with plaster applied over horizontal wood strips or *lath*. Newer homes use sheets of *drywall*. Walls also contain wiring, plumbing, and other utilities that run between the studs.

are covered with lath (wood strips) and plaster. Walls inside newer homes are usually covered with plasterboard, or *drywall*. (SEE FIGURE 1-2.) Other common wall coverings include siding, paneling, and wainscoting. (SEE FIGURE 1-3.)

In addition to the framework and coverings, walls also contain utility runs — plumbing, heating ducts, electrical wiring, phone and TV cables — that you must locate before you begin work. You don't want to accidentally drive a nail or screw into a plumbing or a wiring run.

1-3 In addition to plaster and drywall, inside walls may also be covered with wooden paneling or wainscoting. Paneling normally stretches from the floor to the ceiling; wainscoting usually runs from the floor midway up the wall. In the room shown, the entire wall is covered with drywall, then the wainscoting is applied over it.

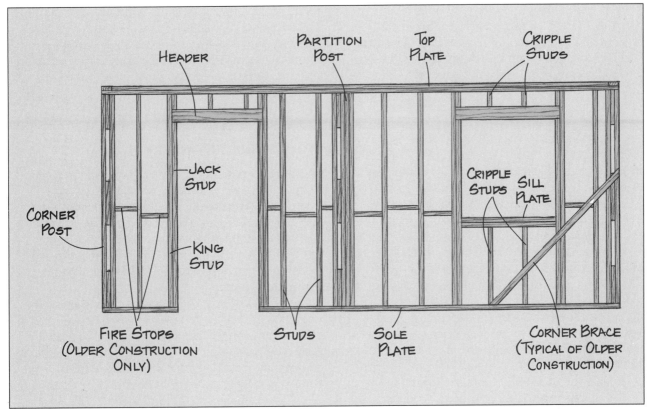

HEADER

PARTITION POST

TOP PLATE

CRIPPLE STUDS

JACK STUD

CRIPPLE STUDS

SILL PLATE

CORNER POST

KING STUD

FIRE STOPS (OLDER CONSTRUCTION ONLY)

STUDS

SOLE PLATE

CORNER BRACE (TYPICAL OF OLDER CONSTRUCTION)

1-4 You cannot simply cut a hole in a wall and insert a window or door — the weight of the materials above the opening must be properly supported to avoid collapsing and crushing whatever you've installed in it. Consequently, door and window openings are spanned with a wide *header* that transfers the load to paired *jack* and *king studs*. In a window opening, there is a *sill plate* at the bottom, supported by *cripple studs*.

Windows and doors — The windows and doors in most homes are manufactured off-site and installed in openings in the frame. These openings are designed to transfer the load generated by the weight of the house to the surrounding frame members so the window and door units won't be crushed. (*SEE FIGURE 1-4.*)

The windows and doors themselves are installed or hung in boxlike jambs or cases. Each case, along with its window or door, is secured in the frame opening as a single unit. (*SEE FIGURE 1-5.*)

1-5 Windows and doors are rarely built or hung on the job site. Instead, they usually come from a manufacturer ready to install, hung in a boxlike jamb or *case*. Each case, along with its window or door, is installed in the frame opening as a single unit. Unless you opt to make your own doors and windows (or recycle old ones), there's little need to build jambs or hang doors and windows.

Floors and ceilings — Floors and ceilings are supported by horizontal frame members called *joists*. Because floors must support a great deal of weight, they are usually built up in two or three layers. First, the rough flooring or *subflooring* is nailed to the joists. Certain types of flooring require a smooth base with as few seams as possible. For these floors, sheets of plywood or particleboard *underlayment* are installed over the subflooring. When a vapor barrier is needed, *builder's paper* is installed over the subflooring or the underlayment. The *finish flooring* is always the last layer when installing a wooden floor. (*See Figure 1-6.*)

Ceilings are much simpler. In older homes, the joists are covered with lath and plaster, just like the walls. In newer construction, builders hang ³/₈-inch-thick drywall from the joists. This material is thinner and lighter than the drywall used for walls.

Moldings and trim — Decorative trim may be attached to the walls, ceilings, floors, and cases around windows and doors. Some trim, such as baseboards and window casements, cover the seams between two surfaces. Baseboards, for example, hide the seam between the flooring and the wall covering. Casements (or *architraves*) disguise the joint between the wall covering and jambs. Trim also enhances the appearance of the finished room. Baseboards provide a pleasing transition between floors and walls; casements make a visual frame for windows. Depending on the type of molding and how it's used in a room, trim can add visual interest; divide the room into areas; or make it seem larger or smaller, more formal or casual, more traditional or contemporary. (*See Figure 1-7.*)

FINISH CARPENTRY TOOLS
WOODWORKING ON SITE

You can accomplish most finish carpentry projects with ordinary woodworking and carpentry tools. There are a few special finish carpentry tools, but, by and large, most tools will be familiar to woodworkers. The one difference is that some work won't be done in the shop, so you may want to invest in a few portable tools that will enable you to do fine woodworking on the job site.

One of the most versatile on-site tools is a power miter box or *chop saw*. (*See Figure 1-8.*) This saw makes quick, clean cutoffs and miters, and can be used for both rough and finish work. If you don't need all the capabilities of a chop saw, consider a traditional hand-powered *backsaw* and miter box. (*See Figure 1-9.*) Although these won't handle all the jobs a chop saw will, they pair up to make a good cut-off and mitering tool for trim work.

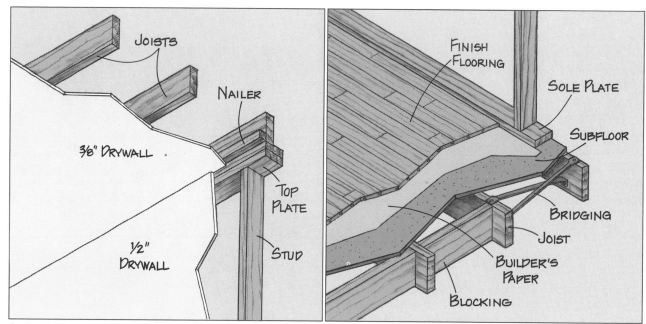

1-6 Ceilings and floors are attached to the joists. Most ceilings consist of a single, thin layer of drywall or plaster and lath, nailed or screwed to the undersides of the joists. Floors must support a great deal of weight, and usually are built up in layers on top of the joists.

1-7 These rooms from two homes show radically different approaches to trim, with different effects. In the entranceway of the traditional Victorian home (*left*), the trim is a predominate visual element, framing the windows and doorway. In the contemporary entranceway (*right*), the trim is much more modest and does not dominate.

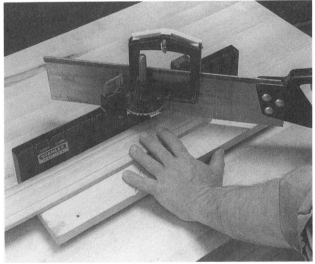

1-8 A power miter box is also known as a *chop saw* because the blade swings down and seems to chop the board in two. But don't let the name fool you — when properly aligned and adjusted, a good chop saw is an extremely accurate cutting tool. Look for a saw with a large capacity that can make *compound* as well as simple miters. The saw shown is a *sliding* miter saw — it not only swings down but travels horizontally several inches. This increases the cutoff capacity.

1-9 If you enjoy working with hand tools, use a *backsaw* and a *miter box* for cutting trim. These are not as quick or as versatile as a chop saw, but a good set can be just as accurate. Sharpen the saw (or have it sharpened by a professional service) before you use it. With few exceptions, manufacturers just stamp and set the teeth of new handsaws; they don't grind them. A backsaw will cut cleaner and quicker once the teeth are ground.

When you need to shave a board to adjust the fit, a hand-held *power plane* saves time and effort. *(SEE FIGURE 1-10.)* There's no substitute for traditional block and bench planes when you need finesse, but if you have a lot of planing to do, a power plane is quicker and easier.

A *router* and a *router table* are indispensable if you make your own moldings. *(SEE FIGURE 1-11.)* The router table should be small and lightweight so you can move it around easily.

You may also want to consider bringing a bench-top band saw or scroll saw right into the house. *(SEE FIGURE 1-12.)* Both of these do the work of a coping saw, cutting shapes and coping joints.

Many finish carpentry projects require that you locate studs and joists in a room. An electronic *stud finder* lets you see through drywall, plaster, and paneling, finding the frame members without having to remove the wall covering. *(SEE FIGURE 1-13.)* Some newer stud finders use low-power radar to locate wiring and plumbing runs as well as framing members.

Finally, you might want a few aids to help you work up high or down low. In your workshop, most of the work is at waist level; on a job site, you frequently have to work close to the floor or ceiling. A pair of *knee pads* saves wear and tear on your anatomy when working low, and a sturdy *stepladder* is essential for reaching the high places. *(SEE FIGURE 1-14.)*

1-10 **When you need to trim** stock from a wooden surface, a *power plane* can be a real boon. Block and bench planes will work well, but a power plane is quicker and requires less effort. Additionally, a power plane is easier to use when the workpiece is difficult to reach or oddly positioned. To use a traditional plane effectively, you must be able to brace yourself to push the plane across the board. Not so with a power plane. Because the rotary knives do the work, all you have to do is guide the tool across the wood surface.

1-11 **If you make your own** moldings and trim, a *router* is an indispensable tool on the job site. It also helps to have a *router table* so you can use the router as both a stationary and a portable tool. The table should be small enough to move easily, or you can build this "Folding Power Tool Stand." (See page 95 for plans and instructions.) This fixture is designed to mount a router, chop saw, and saber saw.

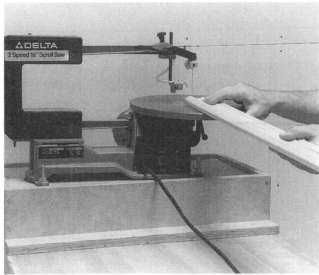

1-12 The traditional finish carpenter's tool for cutting shapes is a *coping saw*. However, you can perform the same operation with less effort if you bring a benchtop *band saw* or *scroll saw* to the job site. If you use a scroll saw, outfit it with a spiral saw blade. Spiral blades cut in all directions. This enables you to cut complex shapes in long boards without having to turn the workpiece.

1-13 As long as the material covering the walls and ceilings isn't too thick or dense, an electronic *stud finder* is a reasonably accurate way of locating the frame members in walls and ceilings. This particular stud finder can be adjusted for the thickness of the wall covering (up to about 1 inch). **Note:** Once you've found two studs or joists, it's a cinch to find the rest. Measure the distance between the two, then calculate the approximate location of the remaining frame members. Use the stud finder to pinpoint their positions.

1-14 In addition to ordinary protective gear (safety glasses, dust mask, and gloves), you may also want to invest in a set of *knee pads*. A lot of finish carpentry work is done close to the floor in a kneeling position. Knee pads will protect your knees and shins, allowing you to work longer and more comfortably.

STEPLADDER WORK TRAY

On finish carpentry jobs, you often spend a lot of time on a stepladder. You may also spend a lot of time climbing up and down the stepladder, fetching tools. This bolt-on tray helps to eliminate some of the climbing. It holds a large assortment of tools and materials at waist level, where they're easy to reach as you work.

To make the tray, first calculate how the ladder tapers on *one side*. Measure the width of the ladder (from rail to rail) at the top and the bottom. Subtract the top width from the bottom width and divide by 2 — this is the taper. For example, if the ladder is 24 inches wide at the bottom and 18 inches at the top, each side tapers 3 inches:

$$(24 - 18) \div 2 = 3$$

Next, convert the taper to a slope. Measure the length of the rails. Divide the length in inches by 12 to convert it to feet, then divide this number into the taper to get the slope. If the taper is 3 inches and the rails are 36 inches long, the slope is 1 inch per foot:

$$3 \div (36 \div 12) = 1$$

Cut the wedge-shaped spacers to match the slope of the ladder. Cut the supports long and temporarily clamp the supports and spacers to the ladder rails. Stand on the top step of the ladder. (**Warning:** Don't stand on the *top* of the ladder; this is unsafe. Stand on the *top step* — the level just below the top.) Mark the supports where they are even with your waist. Also measure the distance between them at this point. Remove the supports and spacers from the ladder, cut them to the length you have marked, and build a tray to fasten between the supports.

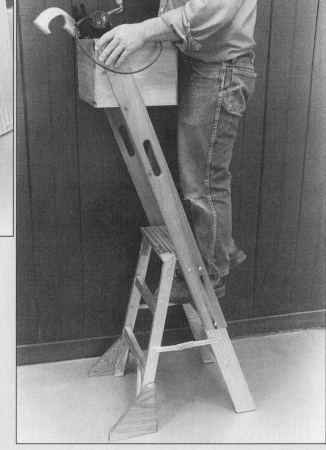

To attach the work tray, drill holes through the supports and the ladder rails, then fasten them together with carriage bolts and wing nuts. Put a few tools in the tray and check if the ladder is top heavy — small ladders may tend to tip forward when the tray is loaded. If the ladder is top heavy, attach leg extensions to the front feet, as shown.

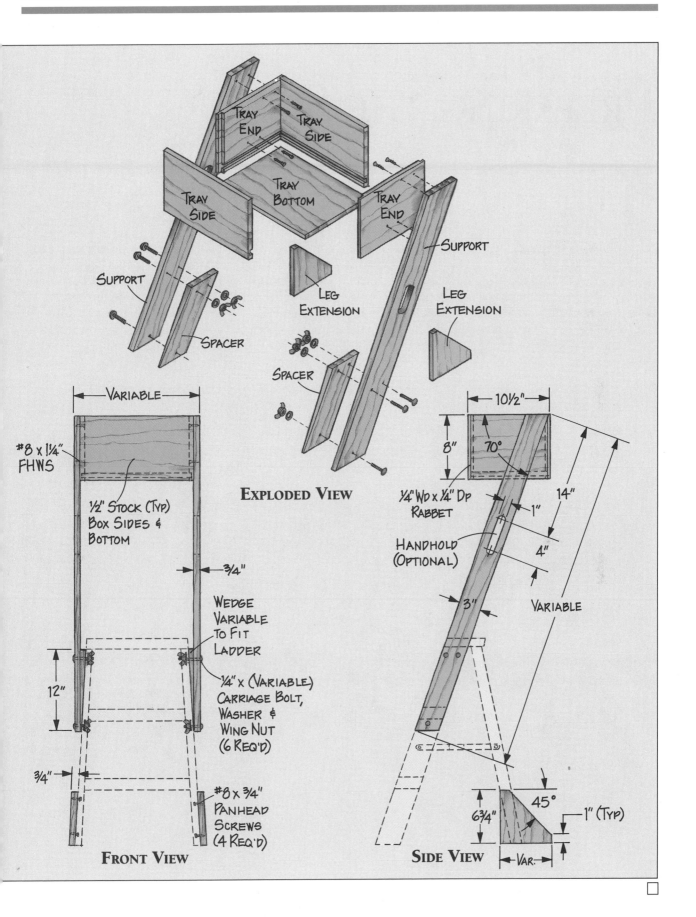

EXPLODED VIEW

TRAY END

TRAY SIDE

TRAY BOTTOM

TRAY SIDE

TRAY END

SUPPORT

SUPPORT

LEG EXTENSION

LEG EXTENSION

SPACER

SPACER

VARIABLE

#8 x 1¼" FHWS

½" STOCK (TYP) BOX SIDES & BOTTOM

¾"

WEDGE VARIABLE TO FIT LADDER

¼" x (VARIABLE) CARRIAGE BOLT, WASHER & WING NUT (6 REQ'D)

12"

¾"

#8 x ¾" PANHEAD SCREWS (4 REQ'D)

FRONT VIEW

10½"

8"

70°

¼" WD x ¼" DP RABBET

14"

1"

HANDHOLD (OPTIONAL)

4"

3"

VARIABLE

45°

6¾"

1" (TYP)

VAR.

SIDE VIEW

2

PREPARING THE SITE

The first step in any finish carpentry job is preparing the job site. Every rough structure requires at least a little touch-up, whether you are finishing a new home or remodeling an older one.

If the house is new, you must check the work of the rough carpenters and true up parts of the structure that might interfere with your finish work. Oversights such as out-of-square door and window openings, crowned or bowed studs and joists, and improperly assembled frame members will cause problems if left uncorrected.

If you're working in an older home, you must undo the ravages of time — rotted sills, sagging floors and ceilings, and framework that is no longer plumb or true. Or, if the house no longer suits your needs or tastes, you will have to modify the structure.

12

REFINING THE STRUCTURE

Before you begin work, evaluate the structure for potential problems. If you're finishing a new home, try to do this *before* the drywall is installed, while you can still see the frame members. It's much easier to correct minor structural mistakes when the structure is visible. Once the walls and ceilings are covered, it may be too late. You'll have to work around these errors, and this will cost you time and frustration.

If you are remodeling an older home, remove the windows, doors, and trim that you intend to replace. Identify the locations of the studs, joists, and all utility runs. Where necessary, remove the wall coverings.

Check the structure with a tape measure, a carpenter's square, and a level to determine if the parts of the structure are plumb, level, square, flat, and flush where they need to be. (*SEE FIGURE 2-1.*) If the framework is uncovered, inspect the joints where frame

members are attached to one another. The problems that you're looking for and what you do about them depend on the specific work that you plan to do.

FOR BEST RESULTS

Don't hesitate to remove old plaster, lath, and other wall coverings. It's a messy job, but it enables you to find and repair framework problems, add utility runs, install insulation and vapor barriers, and mark the precise location of frame members, pipes, ducts, and wires. Because drywall is so easy to install, many finish carpentry jobs in older homes will go quicker if you bite the bullet and strip the site down to the frame at the beginning of the job.

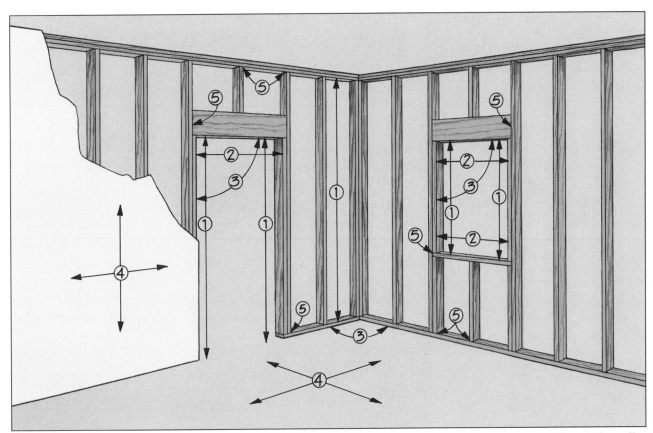

2-1 When inspecting the structure, there are five problems you should look for. Check that the frame members are *plumb, level, square, flat,* and *flush* where they need to be. For example, jack studs and corner posts should be reasonably straight up and down, or *plumb* (1). Headers and subsills must be *level* (2). Door frames, window frames, and corners should be reasonably *square* (3). Floors should be *flat* (4); so should walls when they are covered with drywall or other coverings. The surfaces of frame members should be *flush* (5) where one part joins another.

TRUING THE WALLS

If you plan to install paneling, wainscoting, or trim on the walls, first determine if the walls are flat. Look for studs that are bowed or *crowned* in opposite directions, as well as studs that are crowned more noticeably than others. Also check that the frame members are flush where they join one another. *(See Figure 2-2.)* Both problems will create high and low spots in the walls. This, in turn, makes it more difficult to install wall coverings and trim.

Using a level, check that the corner posts are plumb. If they lean, the walls will not be square. You may not notice the lean if the walls are covered with drywall, but you will if they are covered with paneling or wainscoting — the vertical lines in the wall covering won't be parallel to the offending corner. *(See Figure 2-3.)*

Finally, look for frame members that are cracked or split. Sometimes a large nail will split the end of two-by stock. These fractured parts may work loose and won't properly support the structure above them.

Many of these problems can be solved with a heavy blow from a hammer. For instance, if the edge of a wall stud isn't quite flush with its sole plate, you can move it a fraction of an inch with a hammer blow. *(See Figure 2-4.)* Most structural mistakes, however, require more finesse. When a stud is badly crowned or cracked, you should remove it and replace it with another. Frame members that are not flush and can't be whacked into place need to be shimmed or shaved.

2-2 The edges of this stud are not flush with the sole plate it rests on. Consequently, when the drywall was installed over the framework, it did not remain flat. Instead, it bent to conform to the uneven frame. If you try to install a baseboard over this area, it won't lie flat against the wall. Instead, it will rest at an angle and there will be gaps between the top edge and the wall.

2-3 If one corner of a wall is out of plumb and you cover it with paneling or wainscoting without correcting the problem, the wall covering will have to be tapered to fit the leaning portion of the framework. The vertical lines in the wall will not be parallel with one corner. Oftentimes, this taper won't be noticeable, but if the corner leans too far or the lines in the wall covering are close together, it will stick out like a sore thumb.

WAINSCOTING NOT PARALLEL TO CORNER

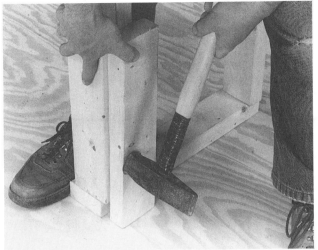

2-4 It's not difficult to reposition frame members that aren't flush with one another. In many cases, one or two good blows with a heavy hammer will correct the problem — the nails will bend slightly and the errant board will move a fraction of an inch without cracking. Place a scrap of wood over the frame member to protect the surface while you hit it. If this doesn't make the framing parts flush, remove the nails, realign the parts, and drive new nails. You can also attach shims to low spots or plane the wood to reduce high spots.

TRY THIS TRICK

Use a *cat's paw* to remove large nails when repositioning or replacing frame members. A pair of *end cutters* works well for small nails.

INSTALLING GROUNDING

For finish carpentry jobs that involve extensive trim, you may want to install *grounding* in the framework — horizontal strips set in notches in the studs. This grounding provides additional anchors for the nails and screws that hold the trim in place. Grounding is especially useful if you intend to add wide baseboards, chair rail moldings, and crown moldings. *(SEE FIGURE 2-5.)* For some types of trim, you can install grounding over the wall covering. *(SEE FIGURE 2-6.)*

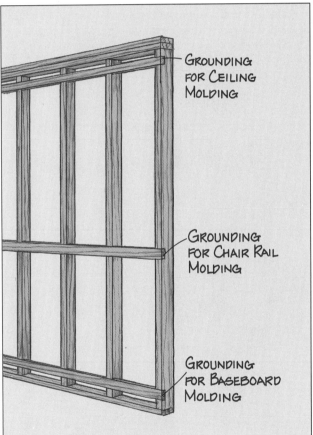

GROUNDING FOR CEILING MOLDING

GROUNDING FOR CHAIR RAIL MOLDING

GROUNDING FOR BASEBOARD MOLDING

2-5 When you plan to install extensive or complex trim, it often helps to add *grounding* to the framework — horizontal wood strips that provide additional support and nailing anchors. Cut notches in the studs at the appropriate height to support the trim, then fasten the strips in the notches. The face of the grounding strips must be flush with the edges of the studs. The wall frame shown has grounding strips for a tall baseboard, chair rail molding, and crown molding.

2-6 You don't always have to
notch grounding into the frame
members. In some cases, you can fasten it directly over the wall or ceiling
covering. These one-by-four strips
are attached to the ceiling over the
drywall. They will provide grounding for a gridwork of beams and
moldings known as a *coffered* ceiling. (See the "Coffered Ceiling" on
page 84.)

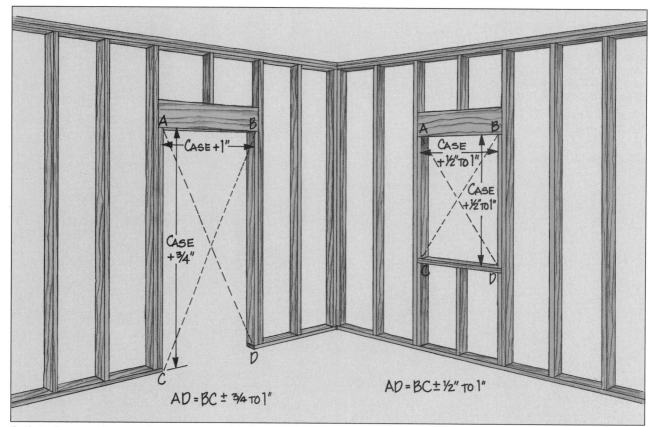

2-7 Before you hang a door or
window, check that the opening is
the proper size. Generally, a window
opening should be ½ to 1 inch wider
and taller than the window frame.
Door openings should be about 1
inch wider and ¾ inch taller than
the door jambs. When you're satisfied the unit will fit, make sure the
opening is square. Measure diagonally from the upper corners of each
opening to the lower ones. Compare
the length of the diagonals — they
should be the same. You can usually
tolerate a window or door opening
that's ¾ to 1 inch out of square,
depending on how the door or window is made, but if the discrepancy
is larger, you will have to move the
framing members to square the
frame.

TRUING DOOR AND WINDOW OPENINGS

If you are installing windows or doors, inspect the structure to prevent problems:

- Measure the openings to make sure they're the proper size.
- Determine that the openings are square. If they aren't, the window and door frames may not be true after they're fastened in place. This, in turn, will prevent the doors and windows from opening and closing properly. (SEE FIGURE 2-7.)
- Inspect the joints between the header, jack studs, and subsill to see that both inside and outside surfaces are flush.
- Test the openings with a level to make sure that the jack studs are plumb and the headers and subsills are level. You can live with a window opening that is slightly out of plumb, but not a door opening. If the jack studs lean, the door will swing open or shut on its own accord.
- Check that the jack studs are properly secured to the king studs so they don't pull loose. (SEE FIGURE 2-8.)

> **TRY THIS TRICK**
>
> Use *pinch rods* to check that door and window openings are square. Select two slender rods, each somewhat shorter than the diagonal distance across the opening. Clamp them together with your hands so they stretch diagonally from one upper corner to the opposite lower corner. Without letting go, see if they'll span the other diagonal. If they're too long or too short, the opening is not square.

To move a frame member, remove the nails that hold it. Reposition the member, check it to be sure the problem is solved, then nail it in place again. (SEE FIGURE 2-9.) If the frame members are not flush and you can't solve the problem by moving them, cut long, tapered wedges and shims to fill in the low spots.

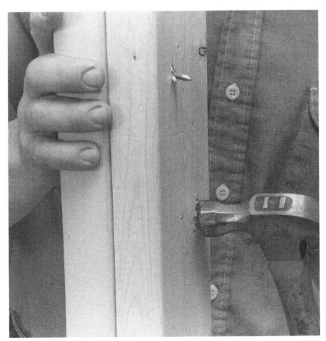

2-8 Jack studs must be properly fastened to king studs, especially if you're installing a heavy door. Either secure them with long screws or drive long nails through both parts and *clinch* them — bend over the pointed ends. Otherwise, the weight of the door may pull the jack studs loose.

2-9 To square a frame opening, remove the nails that hold the misaligned frame member. Reposition the member so the opening is square and fasten it in place again. When leveling headers or straightening jack studs, use wedges to hold them in position as you nail them. In extreme cases, you may have to remove the cripples and cut them (or replace them) before you can level an uneven header or subsill.

LEVELING AND BRACING FLOORS

Before you install flooring, check that the subfloor is level and flat using a string and a level. (SEE FIGURE 2-10.) For this particular job, remember that *flat* is a great deal more important than *level*. It's much easier to fasten flooring to a floor that's slightly tilted than to one that undulates. (SEE FIGURE 2-11.)

What should you do about a floor that's not flat? That depends on the severity of the problem.

■ If there are small variations (less than 1 inch difference between the high and low spots), fill in the low spots with floor leveling compound. (SEE FIGURE 2-12.)

■ If the variations are between 1 and 3 inches, fill in the low spots with particleboard spacers until there's less than 1 inch difference, then apply leveling compound over the particleboard. (SEE FIGURE 2-13.)

■ If there are extreme variations in flatness, as in an older home that has settled unevenly, strip the floor down to the joists. Remove and replace the crooked joists, or nail long, straight scabs to the sides of the joists. (SEE FIGURE 2-14.) When the top surfaces of the floor framing are even, reattach the subflooring.

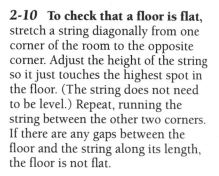

2-10 **To check that a floor is flat,** stretch a string diagonally from one corner of the room to the opposite corner. Adjust the height of the string so it just touches the highest spot in the floor. (The string does not need to be level.) Repeat, running the string between the other two corners. If there are any gaps between the floor and the string along its length, the floor is not flat.

2-11 **To see if a floor is level, first** make sure it's fairly flat. (If it's not flat, there's no sense in checking that it's level. If the surface undulates, some portions will be level and others won't.) Select a long two-by-four that's reasonably straight — *don't* use one that's crowned or crooked. Lay the two-by-four on the floor, resting it on edge. Place a level on the two-by-four and read the bubble. Repeat, moving the two-by-four and level to several different locations.

2-12 To make a floor flat before installing flooring, fill in the low spots with *floor leveling compound*. This is a special mortar mixed with latex to make it slightly flexible. Apply it with a trowel, leveling it as best you can. When the compound hardens, sand it perfectly flat with a belt sander or floor sander. If you must apply the leveling compound to wide areas, install plywood or particleboard *underlayment* over it. You don't want to fasten flooring directly to the compound — it won't hold the nails.

2-13 Floor leveling compound is expensive, so you may want to use particleboard shims to help fill in extremely low spots. In the job site shown, the floor dips over 2 inches in the center. Cut 12-inch-square shims from ¼- and ½-inch thick particleboard. Nail the shims to the low spots in the floor, building them up in layers until they're *almost* even with the high spots. After filling in the low spots as well as possible with shims, spread leveling compound over the entire floor to make it flat.

2-14 If the floor is extremely uneven, you must strip it down to the joists. Stretch strings across the floor perpendicular to the joists and a fraction of an inch above them. Then adjust the strings so they're all at the same height and reasonably level. Nail long, straight lumber (called *scabs*) to the sides of the joists so the top edges are slightly above the joists and just touch the strings. This will keep the scabs even with each other. When you reattach the subflooring, it will be level and flat.

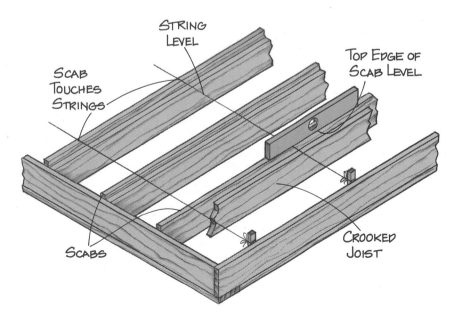

STRING LEVEL

SCAB TOUCHES STRINGS

TOP EDGE OF SCAB LEVEL

SCABS

CROOKED JOIST

You may also have to brace a floor if it bounces or "gives" noticeably when you walk across it. This indicates that the joists are not properly supported. Add blocking between the joists to help distribute the load over a wider area, or brace the joists from below with floor jacks, girders, or shoring. (SEE FIGURE 2-15.)

LOCATING UTILITIES

While you are inspecting the structure, note the location of electrical wires, junction boxes, water pipes, and phone and TV cables. If necessary, measure the positions of the utilities and mark these on a floor plan or an elevation view of the job site.

If you need additional utilities, now's the time to add them. Have an electrician or a plumber install new runs *before* you get to work.

A SAFETY REMINDER

Have your electrician and plumber install metal shields over the wires and pipes where they pass through studs and joists. This prevents you from accidentally driving a nail or screw through them. A misplaced nail could cause an electrical short or poke a hole in a pipe.

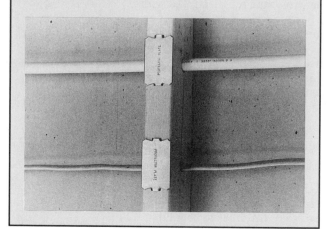

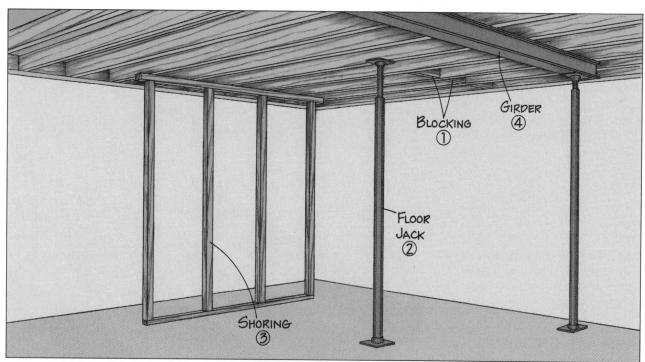

2-15 If a floor has just a little bounce when you walk across it, add **blocking** (1) between the joists. This bracework will distribute the load over a wider area of the floor. If the floor gives noticeably, you must support it from below. Use *floor jacks* (2) to brace small areas and *shoring* (3) for slightly larger expanses. If the entire floor seems weak, install a *girder* (4) under it, perpendicular to the joists.

CHANGING THE STRUCTURE

REDUCING, ENLARGING, AND CREATING OPENINGS

On some jobs, especially remodeling projects, you may have to change the size of a door or window opening — or create a new one. Technically, this is rough or *frame* carpentry rather than finish work, since you're actually rebuilding the structure. You may want to hire out this part of the job to an experienced carpenter, especially if the changes are extensive. It's not difficult work, but it can be time consuming.

The amount of work depends on whether you want to reduce, enlarge, or create an opening. Reducing requires the least work; simply fill in the existing frame opening with studs, jack studs, headers, subsills, and cripples as needed. Cover the framework and insulate it. (*SEE FIGURES 2-16 AND 2-17.*)

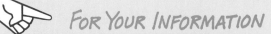

FOR YOUR INFORMATION

In many communities, you must obtain a building permit before making structural changes to your home. Check with your local planning office before you begin.

2-16 To reduce the size of an opening, first remove the existing window or door. Build a new frame within the existing one, adding studs, headers, cripples, and other frame members as needed. The door opening shown is being reduced to hold a window.

2-17 Cover the new framework with materials that match the exterior of your home, but leave the new opening uncovered. Insulate the wall and add a vapor barrier. *Don't* cover the inside surfaces of the frame with drywall or another wall covering — this is best left until after you've installed the door or window.

Enlarging an opening or creating a new one requires more effort. To make an opening in an exterior wall, outline the opening on the inside, then remove the interior wall covering and insulation. If you are enlarging an existing opening, remove the old door or window. (SEE FIGURE 2-18.) Brace the ceiling above the planned opening to prevent the structure from sagging when you cut away the framework. (SEE FIGURES 2-19 AND 2-20.) Cut through the studs and remove them, along with any other frame members that would block the opening. (SEE FIGURE 2-21.) Assemble a new framework for the planned opening. Attach it to the existing frame and the exterior wall covering. (SEE FIGURE 2-22.) Insulate the wall around the opening, then cut through the exterior wall covering, enlarging or creating the opening. (SEE FIGURE 2-23.)

FOR BEST RESULTS

Wait until the last minute, just before you install the new door or window, to cut through the exterior wall. Leave the siding in place as long as possible to protect your home from the weather.

The procedure for enlarging or creating an opening in an interior load-bearing wall (one that supports the structure above it) is similar. You don't have to remove or add insulation, of course, and you can remove the covering from both sides of the wall before you modify the framing.

2-18 Whether you are enlarging an existing door or window opening in a wall or creating a new one, the procedure is the same. First, mark the outline of the new opening on the inside wall and remove the trim, wall covering, and insulation around it. To give yourself room to work, uncover a wider area than the opening will occupy — expose at least one stud on either side. If you aren't sure where the utility runs are or if you want to add new ones, strip the entire wall. If you're enlarging an existing opening, remove the old window or door.

2-19 Before you remove the existing framework, brace the ceiling temporarily. If you cut away load-bearing studs without installing temporary bracework, the portion of the house above the opening may sag.

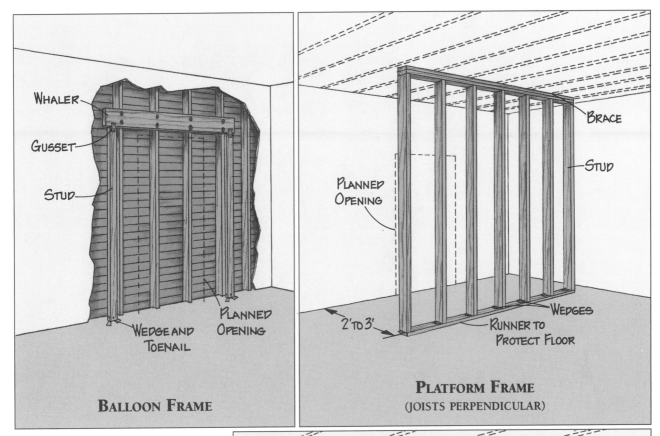

BALLOON FRAME

Labels: WHALER, GUSSET, STUD, WEDGE AND TOENAIL, PLANNED OPENING

PLATFORM FRAME
(JOISTS PERPENDICULAR)

Labels: BRACE, STUD, PLANNED OPENING, WEDGES, RUNNER TO PROTECT FLOOR, 2' TO 3'

2-20 The method for temporarily bracing the ceiling depends on how your home is framed and on the orientation of the ceiling joists. If the house has a balloon frame, fasten a *whaler* to the wall near the top of the studs. Cut two-by-fours to fit snugly between the whaler and the floor. Attach the tops of the two-by-fours to the whaler and wedge the bottoms so they're tight against the floor. If the house has a platform frame and the joists are *perpendicular* to the wall where you will cut the opening, cut two-by stock to make a *brace* that's at least 2 feet longer than the opening is wide. Cut two-by-fours to fit snugly between the brace and a runner on the floor. Attach the tops of the two-by-fours to the brace and wedge the bottoms against the runner. If the joists run *parallel* to the wall, use the same bracework you would for perpendicular joists, but add *cross braces* at the top.

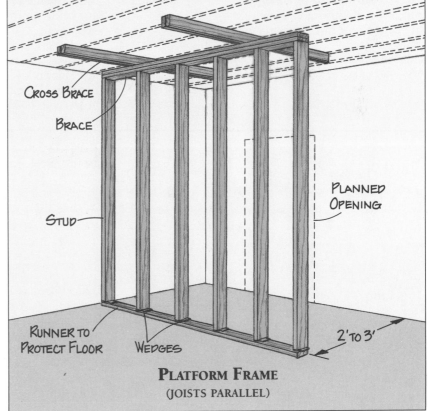

PLATFORM FRAME
(JOISTS PARALLEL)

Labels: CROSS BRACE, BRACE, STUD, RUNNER TO PROTECT FLOOR, WEDGES, PLANNED OPENING, 2' TO 3'

2-21 When the ceiling is properly braced, cut through the old studs where necessary, turning them into cripples. Carefully pry the lower portions of the studs loose from the exterior siding and remove them.

2-22 Install a new framework — king studs, jack studs, header, subsill, and cripples, as required. Make sure that the jack studs are plumb, the header and subsill are level, and the framework is reasonably square. Also check the size of the opening in the frame to make sure the door or window will fit. If you plan to add utilities, have a plumber and/or electrician add new runs. Then insulate the frame around the opening.

2-23 Wait until the last possible minute to create the hole in the exterior wall — leave the siding in place as long as possible to help protect your home from the elements. When you're ready to install the door or window, cut through the siding with a reciprocating saw or circular saw.

3

INSTALLING DOORS AND WINDOWS

Finish carpenters once built windows and doors on the job site, but that time is long past. For over a century, the windows and doors in most American homes have been built off-site by manufacturers who specialize in *millwork*. Ready-made doors and windows arrive at the job already installed in jambs or cases, often with exterior moldings attached as well. All you have to do is fasten these prehung door and window units in the proper openings and attach the interior trim.

It's not quite that easy, of course. You must adjust the unit plumb and square so the window or door operates properly. The jambs must be flush with the interior and exterior walls so the moldings will fit as they should. If you're installing a door, you must add a latch and a strike plate. Most importantly, the installation must be weatherproof to keep your home warm and dry.

INSTALLING DOORS

DOOR CONSTRUCTION

There are dozens of types of ready-made doors, but most can be grouped into just four categories:

■ Slab or *solid-core doors* are wide boards laminated from strips of solid wood. These are most often used as exterior doors — entrances and exits to your home. (*SEE FIGURE 3-1.*)

■ *Hollow-core doors* are made from thin sheets of plywood glued to a frame. This lightweight construction is suited for interior doors between rooms and hallways inside a home. (*SEE FIGURE 3-2.*)

■ *Paneled doors* are built from solid wood using traditional frame-and-panel construction. This construction is suitable for both exterior and interior doors. (*SEE FIGURE 3-3.*)

■ *Metal-clad* and *fiberglass-clad doors* use little wood in their construction. Instead, they're made by covering rigid foam insulation with thin sheets of metal or fiberglass. Oftentimes, fiberglass doors have imitation wood grain that is almost indistinguishable from the real thing. (*SEE FIGURE 3-4.*)

You can purchase all four types of doors prehung in jambs or cases. Each case is a simple box — *side jambs* on the left and right, a *head jamb* above the door, and a *threshold* below it. On most interior door units, there is no threshold, just a temporary cleat nailed to the bottom of the side jambs to keep them properly spaced. (*SEE FIGURE 3-5.*)

Most ready-made doors come predrilled or premortised for hardware. The hinges are already installed and fastened to the hinge jamb. However, you must purchase and install the latch set and the strike plate on the strike side of the door and its case. (*SEE FIGURE 3-6.*)

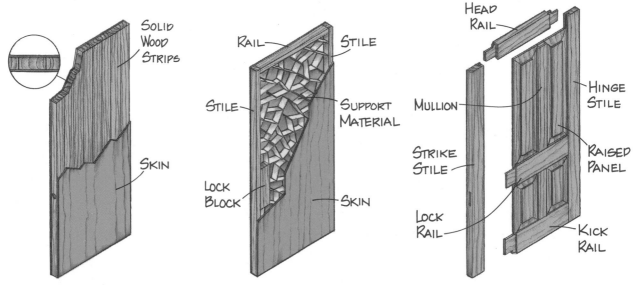

3-1 A *solid-core door* is often just a single wide board, glued up from strips of hardwood and covered on both sides with a thin plywood skin. Each strip in the core is oriented so the radial grain is exposed to minimize expansion and contraction.

3-2 A *hollow-core door* is framed with lightweight *rails* and *stiles*. There is also a solid wood lock block to hold the door latch. The frame is covered on both sides with a thin plywood *skin*. Most of the door is hollow, except for cardboard *support material* that keeps the skin flat and rigid.

3-3 A *paneled door* is built using standard frame-and-panel construction so there are few problems with expansion and contraction. There are at least three rails — the *head rail, lock rail,* and *kick rail*. These are joined to two outside stiles — the *hinge stile* and *strike stile* — with mortise-and-tenon joints. Depending on the design, there may be additional rails and stiles making up the frame. *Raised panels* fill the spaces between the frame members.

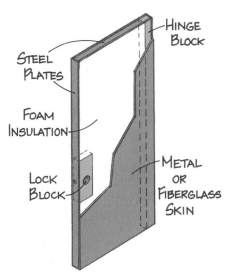

3-4 Metal-clad and *fiberglass-clad* *doors* are built by wrapping a thin metal or fiberglass skin around rigid foam insulation. A wood *lock block* and wood *hinge blocks* reinforce the door where the hinges and the latch are attached.

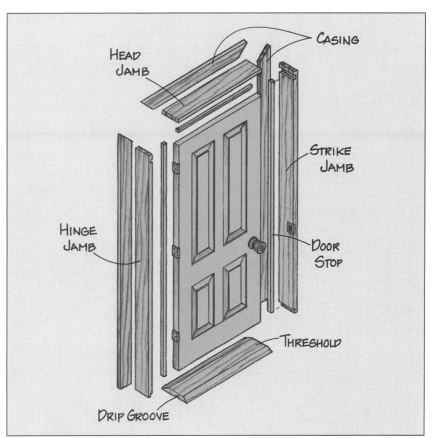

3-5 All four types of doors — solid-core, hollow-core, paneled, and clad — come prehung in ready-made cases. Each case is a simple box consisting of a *head jamb,* two side jambs (a *hinge jamb* and a *strike jamb*), and a *threshold.* (On interior doors, the threshold is usually omitted.) The door closes against *door stops* that are attached to the head and the side jambs. On exterior door units, a *drip groove* on the bottom surface of the threshold keeps rain water from running in under the unit. Many exterior doors come with exterior trim or *casing* already attached to the jambs.

3-6 Although most commercial doors come with the hinges installed, you must install the latch set on the strike side of the door. Usually, the door will be predrilled to accept a standard-size *knob-and-latch assembly* (1), and the jamb will be mortised for a *strike plate* (2). To install a *dead bolt* (3) and the *reinforcing plate* (4) that comes with it, you may have to cut your own mortises in the door and the jamb. Some exterior doors, however, come with precut dead bolt mortises.

If you are modifying or making a new opening for a door, purchase the door *before* you frame the opening. If you are installing the door in an existing opening, be sure it will fit — measure the case before you buy. Doors come in standard heights and widths. Most are 78 inches tall and between 24 and 36 inches wide. Sliding door and atrium door units are commonly available up to 72 inches wide. Also consider whether you need a *right-handed* or a *left-handed* door. (*SEE* FIGURE 3-7.)

Door jambs come in two different widths to fit both old and new construction techniques. Jambs that are 4⁹/₁₆ inches wide will fit new homes that have walls covered with drywall. Jambs that are 5⁵/₁₆ inches wide will fit older plaster-and-lath walls. Be sure to order the proper size. If you are unsure what size you need, buy the smaller one. You can always extend the jambs with wood strips to fit deeper openings. **Note:** If your home is framed with two-by-sixes, you will have to install jamb extensions, no matter what size case you buy.

FOR BEST RESULTS

When purchasing exterior doors, look for *adjustable* thresholds. These let you adjust the level of the threshold after installing the door for a weatherproof fit.

INSTALLING A PREHUNG DOOR

Before installing a prehung door unit, it's wise to double-check the dimensions — make sure the case will fit the opening with a little room to spare. Also check that the door opens in the proper direction, and that the bottom of the door will clear the floor or carpet after it's installed.

If the door swings the wrong way, exchange it for a unit that's hinged on the opposite side. If an *interior* door won't clear the floor covering, remove the door from the case and trim a little stock from the bottom edge. To solve the same problem for an exterior door, remove the framing nails that hold the header and raise it to the height needed. Install a wood spacer at the bottom of the frame opening — this will raise the door unit. **Note:** Do not shorten a prehung exterior door. If you cut stock from the bottom edge, there will be a gap between the door and the threshold.

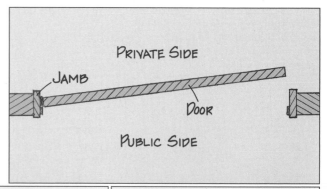

3-7 The way in which a door is hinged determines the *private side* and the *public side* of the door. The door swings toward the private side and away from the public side. Normally, exterior doors are mounted so they open to the inside — the *private* side faces the inside of the home. The placement of the hinges also determines whether a door is *left-handed* or *right-handed*. If the hinges are on the left as you face the public side, the door is left-handed. If they are on the opposite side, it's right-handed.

LEFT-HANDED   **RIGHT-HANDED**

To hang the door, first place the unit in the opening. (SEE FIGURE 3-8.) Insert shims between the side jambs and the frame opening to square the case in the opening. On the hinge side, place the shims directly behind or as close as possible to the hinges. (SEE FIGURE 3-9.)

Once the case is square, make sure the edges of the jambs are flush with the walls. If you are installing an exterior door in a house with exterior sheathing, the public (exterior) edges of the jambs must be flush with the sheathing. On older homes without sheathing,

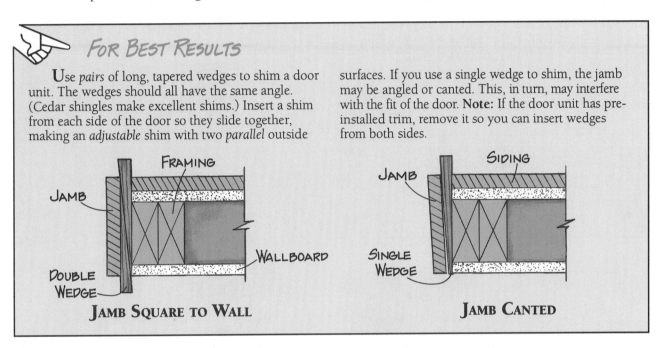

FOR BEST RESULTS

Use *pairs* of long, tapered wedges to shim a door unit. The wedges should all have the same angle. (Cedar shingles make excellent shims.) Insert a shim from each side of the door so they slide together, making an *adjustable* shim with two *parallel* outside surfaces. If you use a single wedge to shim, the jamb may be angled or canted. This, in turn, may interfere with the fit of the door. **Note:** If the door unit has pre-installed trim, remove it so you can insert wedges from both sides.

JAMB SQUARE TO WALL

JAMB CANTED

3-8 To set a door unit in the frame opening, first fit the threshold (or the bottom of the jambs) in the bottom of the opening. Let the door rest on the threshold and lift up on the head jamb, pivoting the unit up and into the opening. Do not force the door.

3-9 Remove the trim from the door jambs, if necessary. Insert shims between the side jambs and the framing to square the unit in the opening. Shim the hinge jamb first, making sure it's plumb. Position the shims behind the hinges. Next, check that the hinge jamb is square to the head jamb. If it's not, insert shims under one of the side jambs to square it. Last, shim the lock jamb. Do *not* insert shims between the head jamb and the header.

the jamb edges should be flush with the siding. For inside doors, the jamb edges should be flush with the wall covering.

Fasten the side jambs to the jack studs. Secure the hinge jamb in place first, driving screws or nails through the jamb and shims in the vicinity of the hinges. Close the door and check the alignment of the lock jamb and the fit of the door in the case. Adjust the shims if necessary, then nail through the lock jamb and shims into the frame. (SEE FIGURE 3-10.) **Note:** When securing the jamb, the nails or screws must go through the *shims* and into the framing.

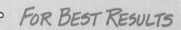

FOR BEST RESULTS

Do *not* fasten the head jamb to the header. If the header settles or warps, it will affect the fit of the door in the case.

If you're installing an exterior door, position the molded door casing on the public (exterior) side and fasten it to the wall with galvanized casing nails. Make a drip cap from aluminum flashing to cover the head casing — this will protect it from the weather and keep water from running down behind the door. (SEE FIGURE 3-11.) Fill the voids between the jambs and the

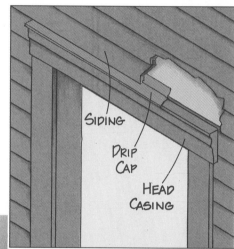

SIDING
DRIP CAP
HEAD CASING

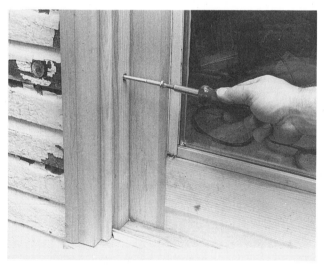

3-10 Check that the edges of the jambs are flush with the sheathing or wall covering. To secure the door unit, drive casing nails or screws through the side jambs and shims and into the jack studs. Fasten the hinge jamb first and check that the door opens and closes easily. Then fasten the lock jamb. **Note:** If you use nails, drive them through, or in front of, the door stops. Don't drive them all the way home — leave ¼ to ½ inch sticking up until you're sure that the door opens and closes properly. Then drive the nails in and set the heads.

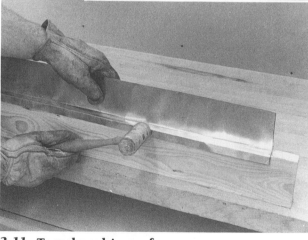

3-11 To make a drip cap for an exterior door, cut a length of aluminum flashing as long as the head casing and about 4 inches wide. With a metal awl, scribe two lines parallel to the long edge of the flashing. Use a scrap of wood with a sharp edge to make 90-degree bends in the flashing along both lines, creating an S-shaped profile. Fasten the drip cap over the casing — it should conform to its shape. If you can, slide the flashing underneath the siding when you install it. Otherwise, caulk the top edge of the drip cap.

frame with insulation, but don't pack it too tightly. (*SEE FIGURE 3-12.*) **Note:** If your home is sheathed, the siding should butt against the edge of the casing. If it's sided with thick, old-fashioned clapboard but has no sheathing, install the casing so it overlaps the siding.

Install the latch set and adjust the strike plate to hold the door against the stops or the weatherstripping when the door is latched. (*SEE FIGURE 3-13.*) If the door has an adjustable threshold, adjust it so the bottom of the door is sealed when shut.

3-12 Weatherproof exterior doors by attaching the exterior casing to the jambs and the house with galvanized casing nails. Apply silicone-based caulk between the siding and the casing to create a waterproof seal. Fill the voids between the door jambs and the frame with fiberglass insulation or low-expansion foam to prevent drafts and heat loss.

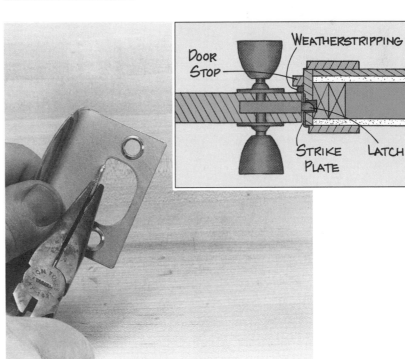

3-13 Install the latch in the predrilled mortises in the door. (Most prehung units are drilled for standard-size hardware; a few are mortised for special hardware that must be purchased from the manufacturer.) Fasten the strike plate in the lock jamb. This plate must be positioned to hold the door snug against the door stop (or the weatherstripping), but not so tight that it's difficult to close. Make small adjustments by bending the tongue inside the strike plate. **Note:** Some strike plates have moveable tongues.

HANGING A DOOR

If you want to build a jamb for an existing door, join
the head jamb and the threshold to the side jambs,
then install the assembly in the frame opening as you
would a ready-made door case. *(SEE FIGURE 3-14.)* If you
already have a jamb in place and want to hang a new
door from it, cut the door to fit the opening, beveling
the edges a few degrees toward the public side. *(SEE
FIGURES 3-15 AND 3-16.)*

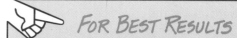

FOR BEST RESULTS

If you build your own door case, cut the mortises in the hinge jamb *before* you assemble it. This
is much easier than trying to mortise the case after
it's installed.

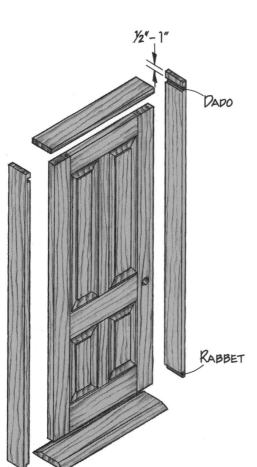

3-14 To make a door case, join
the head jamb and the threshold to
the side jambs with dadoes and rabbets, as shown. Cut dadoes 1/2 to 1
inch from the top edges of the side
jambs and rabbet the bottom edges.
If there is no threshold, omit the rabbets and temporarily nail a spacer to
the edges of the side jambs to keep
them the proper distance apart until
they are installed. Install the case in
the opening, shimming the side
jambs so they're plumb and square
to the head jamb.

3-15 If the door must be sized to
fit the case, remove the door stops
and the casing. Lean the door against
the private side of the opening (the
side that the door opens into). Using
spacers or wedges, position the door
3/4 to 1 inch above the floor and
centered from side to side. Adjust a
compass so the point is 1/16 inch from
the scribe. Hold the compass point
against the jambs while you trace the
opening on the door with the scribe.
(The marks will be the same shape
as the opening, but 1/16 inch smaller
all the way around.) Have a helper
hold the door firmly against the
jamb as you do this.

When the door fits the opening, cut hinge mortises in the hinge stile. Calculate the hinge *backset* — set the hinge back in the door (if necessary) so the door will clear the jamb and the casing when you open it. *(SEE FIGURE 3-17.)* Also, make a "storystick" to lay out the vertical locations of the hinges. If the jamb already has hinge mortises cut, hold the stick up to the jamb and transfer the hinge locations to it. If you must cut hinge mortises on the door *and* the jamb, lay out the hinge locations on the storystick and use the stick to mark both parts. *(SEE FIGURE 3-18.)* **Note:** The hinge mortises on the jamb should be ⅛ inch *below* those on the door — this will create a ⅛-inch clearance between the door and the head jamb and prevent the top of the door from rubbing on the case.

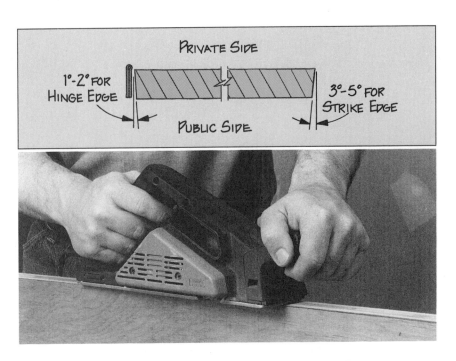

3-16 Cut the door to size. If you need to remove just a little stock, plane the edges until the pencil lines begin to disappear. If you must remove more, saw the door a little wide of the lines, then plane down to them. As you plane, bevel the hinge edge 1 or 2 degrees toward the public side — this will keep the hinges from binding. Bevel the strike edge 3 to 5 degrees so the door will clear the jamb as it opens and closes. After sizing, check the fit of the door in the opening. If it's snug, remove a little more stock with the plane.

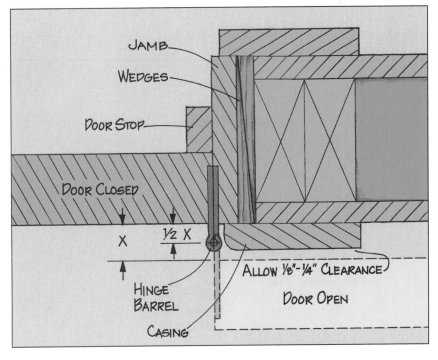

3-17 For a door to open and close properly, the barrel of the hinge must be positioned so the door clears the jamb and the casing when it's open. The pivot point (the position of the barrel) depends on the location of the door in the jamb and the thickness of the casing.

Cut or rout the hinge mortises in the edge of the door (and the jamb, if needed). The depth of the mortises should equal the thickness of the hinge leaves. (SEE FIGURES 3-19 THROUGH 3-21.) Remove the pins to disassemble the hinges. Install the leaves with the fewest knuckles in the door, and those with the most in the jamb. Don't completely tighten the screws in the jamb yet — the hinge leaves should wiggle slightly. To hang the door, align the knuckles on the hinge leaves and insert the pins to lock them together. When all the pins are in place, tighten the loose screws. (SEE FIGURE 3-22.)

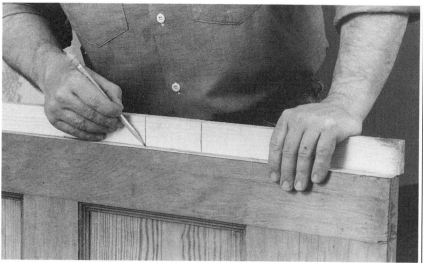

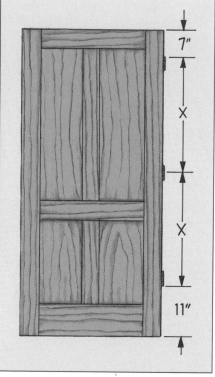

3-18 Normally, the top hinge is 7 inches from the top of the door, the bottom hinge is 11 inches from the door bottom, and the middle hinge is centered between the two. On the jamb, shift the locations down 1/8 inch. Cut a one-by-two the same length as the door and scribe the hinge positions on it to make a *storystick*. When marking the door, align the top end of the storystick even with the top of the door. To mark the hinge jamb, tape a 1/8-inch spacer to the top of the stick and butt the spacer against the head jamb.

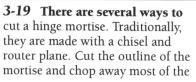

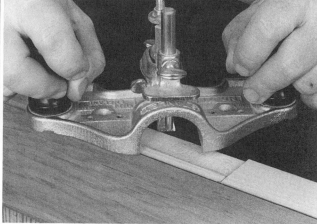

3-19 There are several ways to cut a hinge mortise. Traditionally, they are made with a chisel and router plane. Cut the outline of the mortise and chop away most of the waste with a chisel. Then use a router plane to shave the mortise to the proper depth and flatten the bottom.

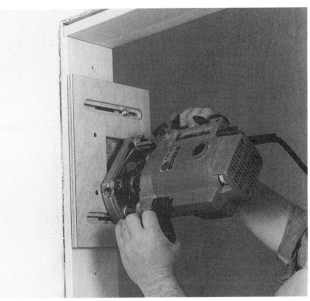

3-20 If you have a lot of hinge mortises to make, it saves time to cut them with a router and a straight bit. (Many door hinges have rounded corners to match the radius of a 1/2-inch straight bit.) Install a guide bushing in the router base and use a template to guide the router as you make the mortise. There are several commercial hinge-mortising templates available, or you can make your own. The shop-made template shown can be adjusted for the backset of the hinge and the thickness of the door. (Refer to *Door-Hanging Fixtures* on page 37 for plans and instructions.)

3-21 If possible, mortise the hinge jamb before installing it. This will be much easier than mortising it in place. If it's not possible and you elect to use a router, temporarily fasten the template to the door jamb with screws. Position the screws so the door stop will cover the screw holes.

3-22 After cutting the mortises, remove the pins from the hinges. Install the leaves with the fewest knuckles in the door and those with the most in the jamb. Don't completely tighten the screws that hold the leaves in the jamb; the leaves should be loose enough to wiggle slightly. Align the knuckles on the bottom hinge leaves, then pivot the door up and swing it closed in the opening at the same time. As you do so, align the knuckles so the remaining leaves mate as the door closes. Install the pins, open the door, and tighten the hinge screws in the jamb.

OTHER POSSIBILITIES

Not all doors swing on hinges, of course. There are folding doors, pocket doors, and sliding doors. Some of these come in a case and are installed like any prehung door unit. Others hang on special hardware supplied by the manufacturer. Ordinarily, these install-ations are relatively simple: Following the manufacturer's instructions, build a jamb and install it in an opening. Attach the door hardware to it, then hang the door from the hardware. (SEE FIGURES 3-23 AND 3-24.)

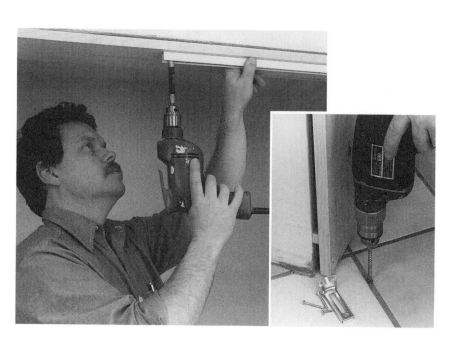

3-23 To install a ready-made folding door, first make a jamb with the recommended inside dimensions and install it in the opening. Following the manufacturer's directions, position the hardware and fasten it in the opening. To hang this particular door, secure the top pivot and the guide rail to the head jamb and mount the bottom pivots to the side jambs and floor.

3-24 After installing the hardware, hang the door. Insert the fixed bottom hinge pin in the bottom pivot. Swing the door up, depress the spring-loaded top hinge pin, and insert it in the top pivot. Also depress the spring-loaded guide pin and insert it in the guide rail. If necessary, adjust the position of the pivots so the door opens and closes properly.

DOOR-HANGING FIXTURES

If you have a lot of doors to hang, these three simple shop-made fixtures will make the task easier. An *adjustable hinge-mortising template* guides a router to cut hinge mortises. It fits any door, no matter what the thickness, and can be adjusted for the proper backset. *Door bucks* hold a door on edge horizontally, allowing you to plane the edges or cut hinge mortises. A *door trimmer* helps you make perfectly straight cuts with a circular saw when trimming a door to size.

1 **To use the *adjustable hinge-mortising template*,** install a ⅝-inch-diameter guide bushing and a ½-inch straight bit in your router. Determine the hinge backset and position the private mount (the mount that's closest to the open side of the template) accordingly. Move the mount *away* from the open side to *increase* the backset and *toward* it to *decrease* the backset. Place the template on the door edge with the private mount against the private side of the door (the same side as the hinge barrels). Position the public mount to rest against the other side, and clamp the mounts to the door. Adjust the router's depth of cut to the thickness of the hinge leaves, then rout the mortise using the bushing and the template to guide the router.

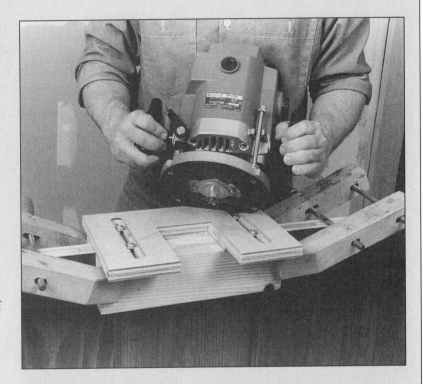

2 **When you rest a door in this *door buck*,** the weight of the door flexes the base, causing the jaws to pinch the door and hold it tight. The jaws on one side of the buck move to accommodate doors of different thicknesses. Fasten the movable jaws in the screw holes closest to the fixed jaws to hold doors between 1 and 1½ inches thick, or move them farther away to hold doors between 1½ and 2 inches thick.

(continued) ▷

DOOR-HANGING FIXTURES — CONTINUED

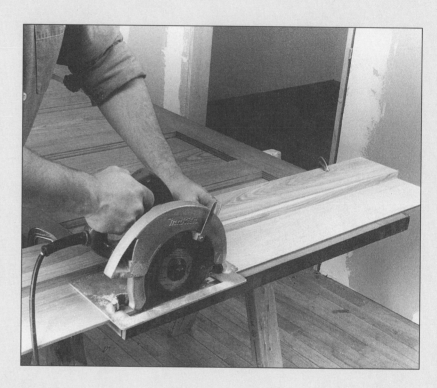

3 **To make the *door trimmer*,** joint the edge of a clear, straight hardwood board and fasten it to a wide strip of ¼-inch plywood. Place a circular saw on the plywood base with the sole against the straightedge. (The saw's electric motor should overhang the straightedge.) Cut the base, keeping the sole pressed against the straightedge. To use the trimmer, clamp it to a door, aligning the sawed edge of the plywood base with the line you wish to cut. As you cut, keep the sole against the straightedge. **Note:** This trimmer will only work with the circular saw and the blade you used to cut the plywood base to width. If you change blades (or saws), make another trimmer.

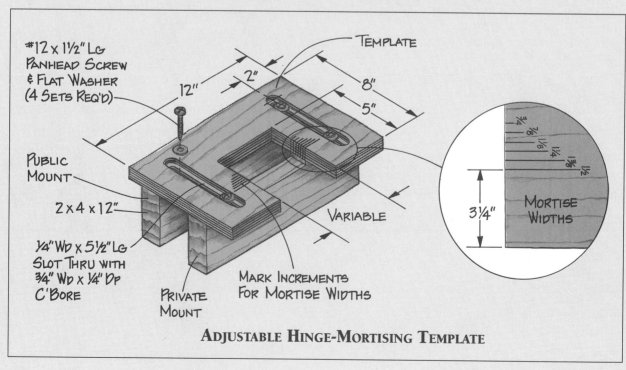

#12 x 1½" LG PANHEAD SCREW & FLAT WASHER (4 SETS REQ'D)

TEMPLATE

12"

2"

8"

5"

PUBLIC MOUNT

2 x 4 x 12"

¼" WD x 5½" LG SLOT THRU WITH ¾" WD x ¼" DP C'BORE

PRIVATE MOUNT

VARIABLE

MARK INCREMENTS FOR MORTISE WIDTHS

¾   ⅞   1⅛   ¼   1⅜   1½

3¼"   MORTISE WIDTHS

ADJUSTABLE HINGE-MORTISING TEMPLATE

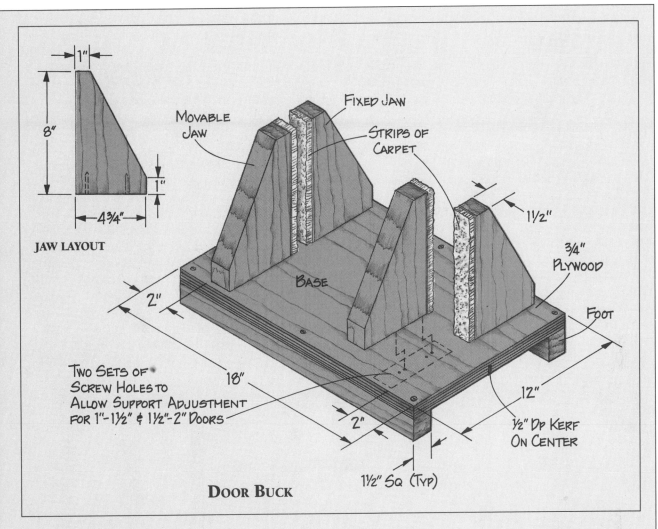

1"

8"

1"

4¾"

JAW LAYOUT

MOVABLE JAW

FIXED JAW

STRIPS OF CARPET

1½"

¾" PLYWOOD

BASE

FOOT

2"

TWO SETS OF SCREW HOLES TO ALLOW SUPPORT ADJUSTMENT FOR 1"–1½" & 1½"–2" DOORS

18"

2"

12"

½" DP KERF ON CENTER

1½" SQ (TYP)

DOOR BUCK

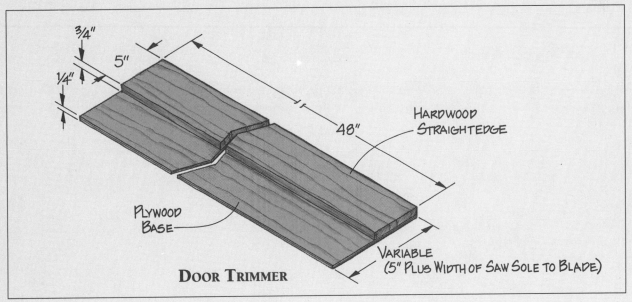

¾"

5"

¼"

48"

HARDWOOD STRAIGHTEDGE

PLYWOOD BASE

VARIABLE (5" PLUS WIDTH OF SAW SOLE TO BLADE)

DOOR TRIMMER

INSTALLING WINDOWS

WINDOW CONSTRUCTION

Most windows consist of panes of glass mounted in frames or sash. The *sash* are hung in a box-like *case.* Windows are categorized according to how the glass is hung. There are many types, but the most common are *(SEE FIGURE 3-25):*

■ *Fixed windows,* in which the panes of glass are fixed in the case and don't open at all

■ *Double-hung windows,* consisting of two sash that slide up and down

■ *Casement windows* with one or two sash that swing open like a door

■ *Sliding windows,* in which the sash slide sideways to open

■ *Awning windows* with one or more sash that open like awnings, with the hinges at the top

■ *Jalousie windows* with many narrow unframed panes that open like awnings (this is one of the few types of windows without a sash)

A window case consists of four parts — two *side jambs,* a *head jamb,* and a *sill.* Depending on how the window is hung, there may also be *stops* and *partition strips* attached to the inside surfaces of the case. Like doors, windows are trimmed inside and out with moldings or *casing.*

Each sash has four frame members — two horizontal *sash rails* and two vertical *sash stiles.* Some windows are divided into several small panes by horizontal and vertical *muntins* within the sash. *(SEE FIGURE 3-26.)*

The window hardware depends on how the window is hung. Casement and awning windows, for example, have pivots and are operated by cranks and gears. A sliding window has guide rails and a latch. The most common type — the double-hung window — has a *balance* to keep the sash in place when they're raised or lowered, and a *sash lock* to secure the sash when the window is closed. *(SEE FIGURE 3-27.)*

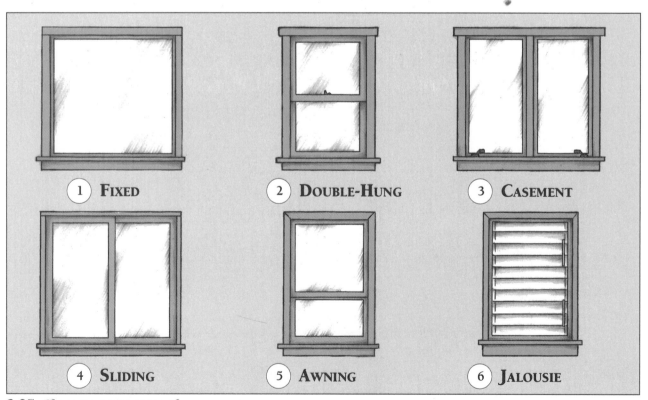

① **FIXED**   ② **DOUBLE-HUNG**   ③ **CASEMENT**

④ **SLIDING**   ⑤ **AWNING**   ⑥ **JALOUSIE**

3-25 There are many types of windows, but the six most common are *fixed* (1), *double-hung* (2), *casement* (3), *sliding* (4), *awning* (5), and *jalousie* (6).

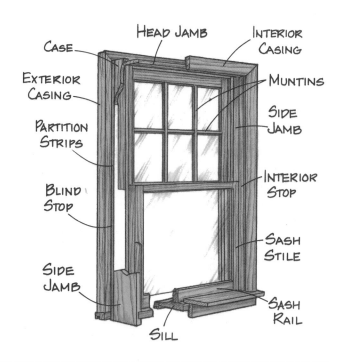

3-26 All prehung windows are installed in *cases,* boxlike assemblies consisting of two *side jambs,* a *head jamb,* and a *sill.* If the window is double-hung, the side jambs will have *blind stops* attached to them near the outside edge, *interior stops* near the inside, and *partition strips* between both sets of stops. These stops and strips guide the windows as they slide up and down. The case is trimmed with interior and exterior *casing.* The glass panes are usually set in frames or *sash.* The sash are made up of *sash rails* and *sash stiles.* If one sash holds several panes, they are divided by *muntins.*

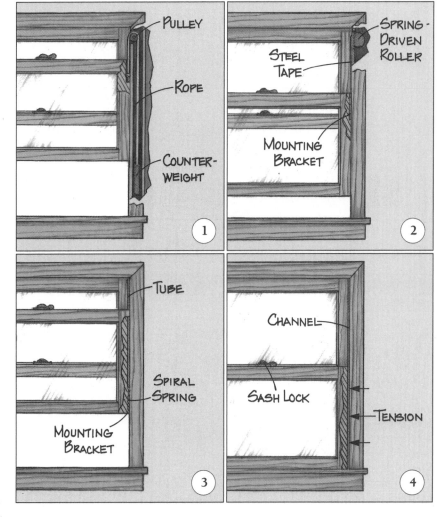

3-27 Double-hung windows use several types of balances — devices for holding sash at any level when you slide them up or down. Many older windows have *block-and-tackle balances* (1) — the sash is attached to ropes which run over pulleys in the side jambs. The other ends of the ropes are attached to counterweights. Old windows may also use *clock-spring balances* (2) — the sash is attached to steel tapes which wind up on spring-driven rollers, like a tape measure. Contemporary windows employ *spiral balances* (3) — the sash is connected to spiral springs. These springs are housed in tubes, which are mounted on the side jambs. Inexpensive windows often rely on a simple *friction balance* (4) — the channels that the sash rides in press against them with enough tension to keep them in place.

INSTALLING A PREHUNG WINDOW

Despite the variety of styles, almost all windows are installed in the same way. The procedure is similar to that for installing prehung doors.

First, check that the rough opening is ½ to 1 inch wider and taller than the window. Also, check that the unit is square. If not, place it on a workbench or flat surface, draw the frame square with pipe clamps, and nail temporary diagonal braces to the side jamb. Trim the braces so they won't interfere with the installation process — they mustn't stick out beyond the case parts or the window won't fit in the rough opening.

Insert the window unit into the rough opening. If the unit comes complete with exterior casing, the casing must overlap the siding or butt against it. If not, the outside edges of the case should be flush with the exterior of the house. (SEE FIGURE 3-28.)

Insert shims between the frame and the window case to hold the window square in the opening. Shim the sill first to level the window, then shim the side jambs. Do *not* insert shims between the head jamb and the header. If the house settles or the header bows, this would distort the window case. (SEE FIGURE 3-29.)

3-28 To set a window in an opening, rest the sill on the subsill and raise the case, pivoting the unit into place. This particular window is being installed so the outside edges of the jambs are flush with the clapboard siding on the house. To do this, tack wood strips across the opening on the outside. Insert the window in the opening from the inside and press it against the strips. **Note:** On newer houses with sheathing, the window would have been set flush with the sheathing.

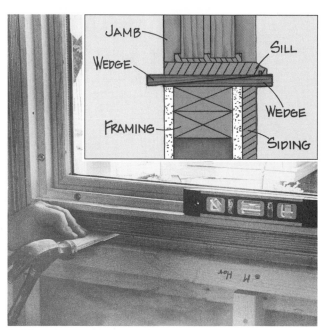

3-29 Check that the window rests level and square inside the opening. If needed, insert shims under the sill to level it. Then add shims between the side jambs and the jack studs, making sure the jambs are plumb and square to the sill. Use a pair of long, tapered wedges for each shim. Insert one wedge from the outside and another from the inside, sliding them together to adjust the thickness. Or, if the window has an exterior casing, slide the wedges together to make a shim of the required thickness and insert it from the inside. Once the window is shimmed, drive casing nails through the case and shims and into the framing. Set the heads of the nails.

Drive casing nails through the case and shims and into the jack studs and the subsill. Some manufacturers recommend that you use window-hanging brackets to install their windows. (*SEE FIGURE 3-30.*) They usually supply these brackets with the window unit when you purchase it.

Once the window is secure, make it weatherproof. If the window is designed to be flashed, cover the gap between the case and the siding with aluminum flashing. (*SEE FIGURE 3-31.*) Fasten the exterior casing to the window case and the house with galvanized casing nails. (*SEE FIGURE 3-32.*) Make a drip cap from aluminum flashing to cover the top exterior casing. Caulk between the siding and the exterior casing, then fill the voids between the window case and the surrounding frame with fiberglass insulation.

FOR YOUR INFORMATION

When installing windows or doors, *don't* use ordinary expanding foam insulation to fill the voids between the frame and the case. This material generates a considerable amount of pressure when it expands in a confined space and it may distort the case, interfering with the fit of the window or door. If you use a foam filler, purchase *low-expansion* foam made especially for this application.

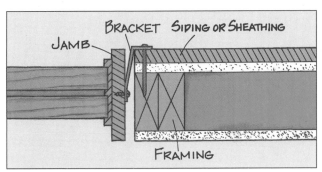

3-30 Some manufacturers suggest using brackets to install their windows rather than driving nails through the case. Attach one end of each bracket to the side jambs *before* you place the window in the opening. Set the window, inserting it in the opening from the outside. Slide it back until the brackets hook over the siding. Fasten the other end of the brackets to the house. Once the exterior casing is installed, it will hide these brackets.

3-31 High-quality windows often have a drip groove all around the outside of the case. An L-shaped flashing hooks in this groove, covering the space between the window and the siding and providing an extra barrier to moisture. You can purchase the flashing from the window manufacturer or make it yourself by scoring flat aluminum flashing parallel to the long edge, then bending it at the score mark. Install the bottom flashing first, then the sides, and finish with the top. The flashings must overlap so they shed water. Seal each flashing in its groove with silicone caulk. Then insert fiberglass insulation from the inside to fill the voids between the case and the framing.

3-32 Once the window is secure, attach the exterior casing to the window case and the siding with galvanized casing nails. Fill the gaps between the casing and the siding with caulk and cover the head casing with a drip cap.

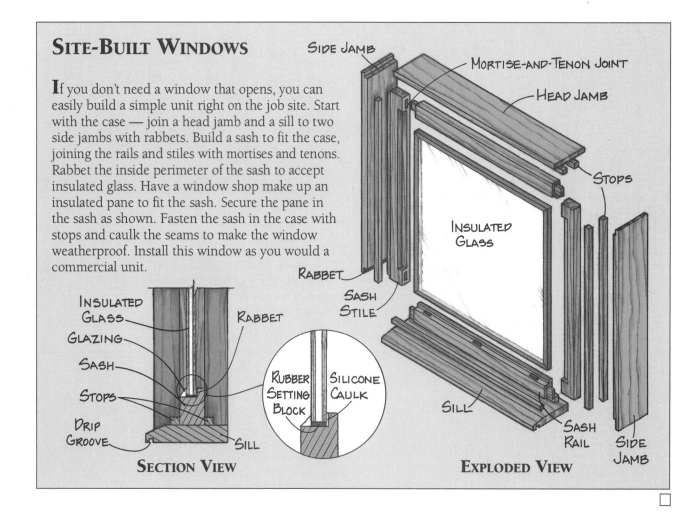

SITE-BUILT WINDOWS

If you don't need a window that opens, you can easily build a simple unit right on the job site. Start with the case — join a head jamb and a sill to two side jambs with rabbets. Build a sash to fit the case, joining the rails and stiles with mortises and tenons. Rabbet the inside perimeter of the sash to accept insulated glass. Have a window shop make up an insulated pane to fit the sash. Secure the pane in the sash as shown. Fasten the sash in the case with stops and caulk the seams to make the window weatherproof. Install this window as you would a commercial unit.

SIDE JAMB

MORTISE-AND-TENON JOINT

HEAD JAMB

STOPS

INSULATED GLASS

RABBET

SASH STILE

SILL

SASH RAIL

SIDE JAMB

INSULATED GLASS

GLAZING

SASH

STOPS

DRIP GROOVE

RABBET

SILL

RUBBER SETTING BLOCK

SILICONE CAULK

SECTION VIEW

EXPLODED VIEW

4

LAYING WOOD FLOORS

Hardwood was once considered the *only* proper flooring. That time is past — hardwood has given way to the expedience of wall-to-wall carpeting and seamless vinyl. But hardwood floors remain a mark of quality in a home.

No other material is so versatile, and few are more durable. When properly installed and finished, hardwood will serve well in any room in the house, from high-traffic kitchens and hallways to less-traveled bedrooms and dens.

If properly cared for, it will outlive the mortgage — sometimes the house itself! It's not uncommon for craftsmen to salvage the hardwood floors from an old house destined for the wrecking ball and give them a new life in another home.

PREPARING THE SUBFLOOR

Just as a house requires a good foundation, a wood floor requires a good subfloor. The best way to prepare the subfloor depends on the type of floor you will lay and how the house is built.

There are three common types of wood flooring — solid wood *tongue-and-groove flooring,* which comes in long strips 3 to 6 inches wide and approximately ³/₄ inch thick; *hardwood plywood flooring,* measuring 2 to 12 inches wide and ¼ to ½ inch thick; and *parquet flooring,* which usually comes in squares 4 to 12 inches on a side and ¼ to ½ inch thick. (Hexagonal and octagonal parquet are also available.)

Tongue-and-groove flooring is strong enough to be applied directly over subflooring. (*SEE FIGURE 4-1.*) Plywood flooring and parquet flooring, however, may require *underlayment* — large sheets of plywood or particleboard fastened to the subflooring. (*SEE FIGURE 4-2.*) Otherwise, the subflooring cannot properly support the thin materials and they will wear quickly. In addition, irregularities in the subflooring will "telegraph" through the flooring, ruining its appearance. Check the recommendations of the flooring manufacturer if you are unsure whether to install underlayment.

4-1 Solid wood tongue-and-groove flooring can be attached directly to properly prepared sub-flooring. Go over the subflooring with a drum sander and 36-grit sandpaper to eliminate any high or low spots. If the floor is directly over a concrete slab, crawl space, or basement, cover it with builder's paper or 6-mil plastic to provide a vapor barrier.

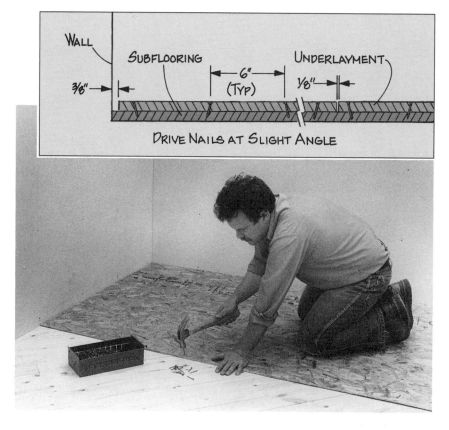

4-2 Plywood and parquet flooring often require *underlayment* — sheets of plywood or particleboard laid over the subflooring to smooth out irregularities and provide additional support. To install underlayment, first cover the subflooring with a vapor barrier, if one is required. Cut the underlayment and lay it in place, leaving ¹/₈-inch-wide gaps between the sheets themselves, and ³/₈-inch-wide gaps between the underlayment and the walls — this will allow for expansion and contraction. Fasten the sheets to the subflooring with nails or screws, spacing the fasteners no more than 6 inches apart. If you use nails, drive them at slight angles, reversing the angle with each nail. This will prevent the underlayment from working loose.

You will need to protect your wood flooring from excessive moisture and condensation. When the floor is directly over a concrete slab, crawl space, or basement, cover the subflooring with 6-mil plastic or builder's paper. (Floors above the first story need no vapor barrier, but you may want to install one anyway to reduce squeaking.) Vent crawl spaces and basements if they aren't already. If the crawl space or basement has a dirt floor, put down another vapor barrier on top of the dirt. (SEE FIGURE 4-3.)

Before installing wood flooring over a concrete floor, check the flooring manufacturer's recommendations. Some types of flooring can be fastened directly to concrete with a thick application of adhesive. Others require that you install a vapor barrier and underlayment. (SEE FIGURE 4-4.)

FOR BEST RESULTS

Always leave a ³/₈-inch-wide gap between the walls and wooden flooring materials to let the floors expand and contract, even if you install a vapor barrier. These barriers only reduce the moisture from the ground; they don't protect the floors from changes in relative humidity.

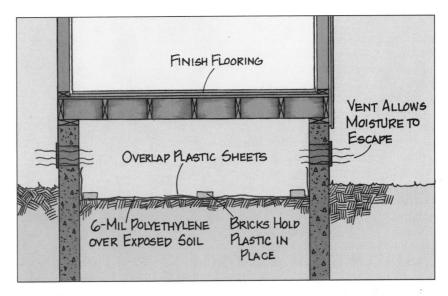

4-3 Basements and crawl spaces with dirt floors often allow moisture to condense underneath floors above. To reduce this condensation, make sure these spaces are properly vented. Also, install sheets of 6-mil plastic over the dirt and weight it down with bricks — this will serve as a vapor barrier to keep some of the moisture out.

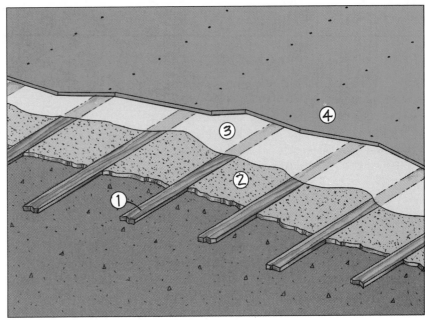

4-4 To prepare a concrete floor for wood flooring, secure nailing strips or *screeds* (1) to the concrete with construction adhesive, spacing them 12 inches apart. Pour *mortar* (2) between the screeds and level the surface flush with the screeds. Lay a 6-mil plastic *vapor barrier* (3) over the mortar and nail plywood or particleboard *underlayment* (4) to the screeds.

If the room has already been trimmed, remove the baseboard moldings and cut off the bottom ends of the door casings so the flooring will fit under them. (*SEE FIGURE 4-5.*) Finally, measure the room and draw a scaled layout. You'll need this layout to figure how much flooring material is required, where to start laying the flooring, and how to proceed.

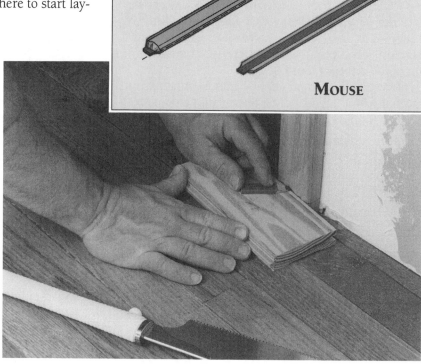

4-5 If you're laying a floor in a room that has already been trimmed, remove the baseboards and shorten the door casings. To determine how much the casings should be shortened, rest a piece of flooring on the subflooring next to the casing. Or, if you plan to install underlayment, rest a piece of flooring on a piece of underlayment and put them both next to the casing. Mark where the flooring meets the casing and cut the casing with a hand saw. **Note:** For marking jobs like this, experienced craftsmen sometimes use a *mouse* — a carpenter's pencil cut in half lengthwise.

INSTALLING THE FLOORING

Tongue-and-groove flooring, hardwood plywood flooring, and parquet flooring each require a different method of installation.

LAYING TONGUE-AND-GROOVE FLOORING

Before you can lay flooring, you must have at least one *baseline* — a reference line on the floor to help keep the flooring strips aligned. Snap a chalk line on the subflooring, vapor barrier, or underlayment, parallel to one wall. (*SEE FIGURE 4-6.*) Measure from this baseline to check the position of the flooring as you lay it.

Finish carpenters sometimes install strips of flooring around the perimeter of a room, parallel to the walls. These decorative *borders* help frame the floor. If you decide to adopt this style, install the borders first, scribing and cutting the outside edges to fit the strips to the walls. (*SEE FIGURE 4-7.*) Leave a small gap (approximately ³⁄₈ inch wide) between the outside edge of the border and the wall to allow for the expansion and contraction of the flooring.

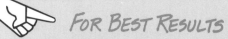

FOR BEST RESULTS

Make sure the *inside* edges of the borders are perfectly straight. It often helps to snap a line for each border and align the wood strips with it.

Lay the first course of flooring parallel to a baseline, with the tongues facing in. Make sure the first course is *absolutely straight*. Nail through the face of the flooring, close to the outside edge, and set the heads of the nails — this is called *face nailing*. Also, nail through the tongues at an angle — this is *blind nailing*, so called because the heads of these nails will be hidden when you lay the next course. (*SEE FIGURE 4-8.*) **Note:** If you haven't installed a border, remember to leave an expansion gap between the wall and the flooring strips.

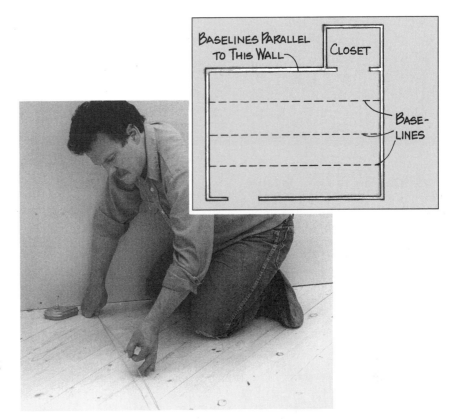

4-6 When laying flooring, you must align the strips with just one wall — usually the wall where you start laying the strips. However, you can't use this wall as a reference; walls are rarely straight enough. Instead, measure partway from the wall into the room. Using a snap line, put down a long, straight chalk line parallel to the wall. (You may want to snap several lines, depending on the size and shape of the room.) Use this *baseline* as a reference when aligning the floorboards.

4-7 If your flooring plan calls for a *border,* install flooring strips around the perimeter of the room. Along the wall where you will start laying the floor, install the border with the *tongue* facing in. Install the other borders with the *groove* facing in. Leave a ³/₈-inch-wide gap between the border and walls to allow for expansion and to compensate for irregularities in the walls. If a wall is more than ³/₈ inch out of true, the baseboards may not completely cover the gap. You will have to cut the border to fit the wall. Lay the border against the wall and sight down the strips to make sure they're straight. Adjust a compass so the distance between the point and the scribe is equal to the largest gap between the wall and the border. Trace the irregularities of the wall with the compass point, scribing the border strips as you do so. Saw or plane the strips to the scribe marks.

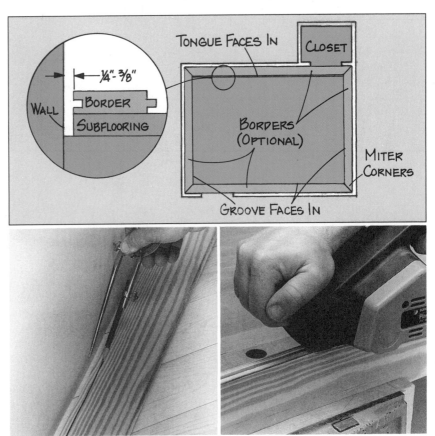

Lay the next course, blind nailing *only*. Offset the ends of the strips at least 3 inches from those on the first course. Before you drive the nails, seat the tongues in the grooves by tapping the strips with a *beater block* and a mallet. (*SEE FIGURE 4-9.*) Lay the remaining courses in the same way. To save time, you may want to start *racking* — laying out several courses at once, then nailing them in place. (*SEE FIGURES 4-10 AND 4-11.*)

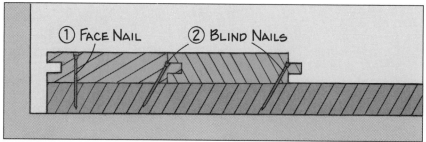

4-8 There are two ways to fasten tongue-and-groove flooring to the subfloor. You can *face nail* (1), driving the nails through the faces of the flooring strips and setting the heads. Or, you can *blind nail* (2), driving nails through the tongue at an angle, where they will be hidden from view when all the flooring is installed.

You can blind nail most of the flooring. You only need to face nail the borders (if there are any), the first course, and the last few courses.

Note: If you have a lot of flooring to lay, you can rent both face nailers and blind nailers from most tool rental services.

4-9 As you lay each successive course of flooring, you must seat the tongues and the grooves together as tight as they will go. To do this, place a scrap of flooring (a *beater block*) against the strip and whack it with a mallet. Slide the beater block sideways a foot or so and repeat until you have seated the entire course. Sight down the course to make sure it's straight and measure from the closest baseline to check that it's parallel. Then blind nail it in place.

4-10 The job goes faster and you get better results if you *rack* several courses at a time before you install them. Select strips from the bundle of flooring and arrange them on the subflooring in the order in which you will install them. Match the grain and the wood tones to form pleasing patterns.

Sight down each course as you beat it into place to check for straightness. Also check that it parallels a nearby baseline. If not, gradually correct the error over several courses. You can also taper flooring strips, if necessary. (SEE FIGURE 4-12.) If you taper a strip, recut the tongue or the groove.

When you have to butt the groove side of flooring strips to the groove side of the borders, install splines between the boards. (SEE FIGURE 4-13.) Also use splines to reverse the direction of the tongues when you must *back lay* flooring into a small area like a closet or an alcove. (SEE FIGURE 4-14.)

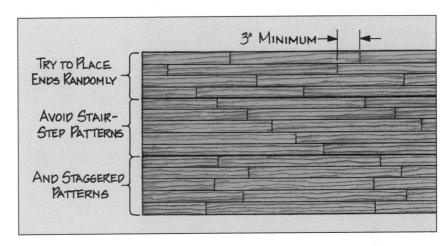

4-11 For strength, the ends of the strips in each course should be offset at least 3 inches from the ends in the previous course. Unless you want to create a precise geometric pattern in the floor, place the ends randomly. Imprecise and partial patterns will be distracting. A random look is easy to achieve when you rack the courses before you install them; it's much more difficult if you lay out and nail only one course at a time.

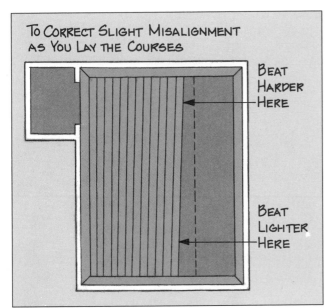

4-12 If you should discover that the flooring is misaligned with a baseline, you can correct the problem over several courses. When seating the flooring, beat the strips a little harder where they are too close to the baseline, and not quite so hard where they are too far away. If the misalignment is extreme or the wall where you end the flooring is not parallel with the wall where you began, saw a taper in the last course.

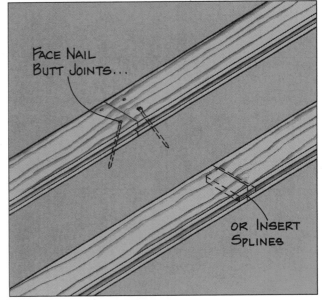

4-13 When you butt flooring strips end to end or against borders, install *splines* between the parts. If you can't use splines, face nail the ends of the boards where they butt against one another. **Note:** Many craftsmen prefer to *back cut* butt joints; that is, make the cut at a slight angle so the top edges of the board meet and form a tight seam.

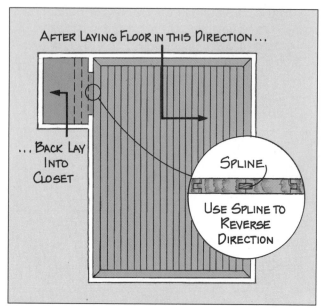

4-14 Occasionally, you must *back lay* flooring in alcoves and closets, reversing the direction in which you were working when you laid the main portion of the floor. This means reversing the direction of the tongues and grooves. Install a spline in the flooring groove where you will start back laying. Use this like a tongue, fitting the groove on the next course to the spline.

4-16 You won't be able to seat the last few flooring courses with a beater block; the wall will be in the way. Instead, seat them by using a pry bar or making a lever and fulcrum from scraps. Place one or more short scraps (the fulcrum) over a wall stud and insert the end of a longer scrap (the lever) between the wall and the last course. Push the lever toward the wall so it pivots on the fulcrum, forcing the flooring strips into place. *Be sure the fulcrum is over a stud when you push, otherwise you will punch through the drywall!* When the space between the wall and the flooring grows too narrow to use this method, rip the last course to the proper width (allowing for a 3/8-inch-wide gap) and lay it next to the last course. Use wooden wedges to seat the tongues in their grooves, then face nail it. *Once again, make sure the wedges are over studs!*

Install *reducers* where the flooring butts against carpet, tile, or flooring of a different thickness. (*See Figure 4-15.*) As you approach the end of the job, face nail the last few courses. Because you'll likely be up against a wall, you won't have room to use a beater block. Instead, push or pull the strips into position with a wood scrap. (*See Figure 4-16.*)

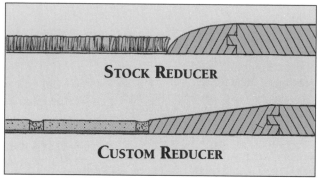

4-15 If the flooring butts against carpet, tile, or wood flooring of a different thickness, install a *reducer* to make the transition smoothly. This is a wedge-shaped piece of flooring that provides a ramp between one level and another. Some manufacturers offer reducers for popular flooring styles; generally, you must make your own.

LAYING HARDWOOD PLYWOOD FLOORING

Like solid wood flooring, hardwood plywood flooring also fits together with tongues and grooves. For that reason, it's installed in much the same way. Lay down baselines and align the plywood strips parallel to them, fitting the tongues and grooves together. Offset the ends on each successive course and try not to let obvious patterns develop.

There are two important differences, however. First, because the plywood strips are thinner than solid wood flooring, the tongues are more fragile. You cannot beat them in place; even a rubber mallet may prove too aggressive when installing thin flooring. Instead, you must slide the strips together with finger-tip pressure only.

Second, you cannot blind nail thin strips; once again, the tongues are too fragile. Plywood flooring is designed to be laid with flooring adhesive or *mastic.* Spread mastic with a grooved trowel, applying enough

for several courses at a time. (*SEE FIGURE 4-17.*) Face nail the first course so it won't shift. For successive courses, press the flooring into the adhesive until it "grabs," then slide the tongues and grooves together. (*SEE FIGURE 4-18.*)

Wait until the mastic sets completely before you walk on the floor or sand it. While the adhesive is still soft, the flooring can easily scoot out of alignment. Depending on the type of adhesive, it may take a day or more to harden completely.

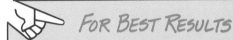

FOR BEST RESULTS

If you must walk on newly installed plywood flooring, lay long planks or sheets of plywood across it. Do *not* step directly on the flooring.

4-17 Most plywood flooring is installed with *mastic,* a special flooring adhesive. Spread a coat on the floor with a grooved trowel and wait a few minutes for the adhesive to *flash* — it will glaze over and feel slightly rubbery. However, don't let it dry out. The adhesive must grab the flooring when you press it in place. If you can't feel it grip, it's too dry. Scrape up the mastic and apply a new coat.

4-18 Lay the courses of plywood flooring in a similar manner to tongue-and-groove flooring. Rack several courses and apply just enough mastic to the floor to lay them. Slide the strips into place, then repeat. As you work, check the position of each course relative to a baseline. If a course is not aligned properly, shift the flooring to bring it back into alignment. The mastic does not set quickly; you can adjust the flooring for several hours.

LAYING PARQUET FLOORING

Like plywood flooring, parquet is laid with mastic. However, because this flooring material comes in small squares rather than long strips, it's more difficult to align. Instead of snapping a single set of baselines parallel to one wall, you must snap *two* sets. If you want to align the rows of parquet blocks with a wall, the first set of lines should be parallel to that wall. If you want to lay them on a diagonal, snap them at a diagonal. (Usually, the diagonal will be 45 degrees, measured from a reference wall.) However you make

the first set, the second set must be 90 degrees from them, making a grid.

Begin laying the parquet in the *center* of the room, starting at a point where two baselines cross. Set the first square so one side is aligned with one baseline and an adjacent side is aligned with another. (*See Figure 4-19.*) Work out from this point, keeping the edges of each parquet squarely aligned with both sets of baselines. (*See Figure 4-20.*)

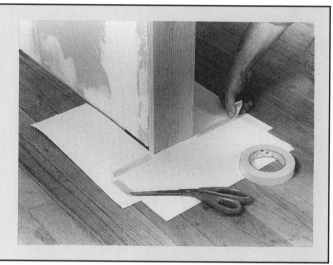

Try This Trick

When you must fit flooring around a shape that cannot be scribed, make a cardboard template. Cut pieces of cardboard or posterboard, fit them around the obstacle, and tape them together so they won't shift. Use this as a template to mark the flooring, then cut the flooring to shape.

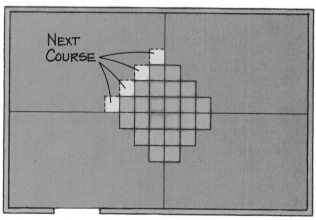

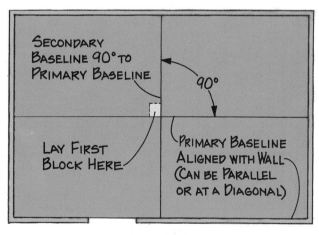

4-19 To lay parquet, snap *two* sets of baselines at 90 degrees to one another. Lay the first piece of parquet in the approximate center of the floor where two baselines cross. Align one edge of the square with one baseline, and an adjacent edge with the other.

4-20 Lay the parquet in an expanding pyramid or diamond pattern around the first piece you installed. Each course will be a *diagonal* row of squares, laid corner to corner. By proceeding in this fashion, it's much easier to keep the courses properly aligned to both sets of baselines.

FINISHING FLOORS

Nowadays, much commercial wood flooring comes prefinished; all you have to do is install it. However, many floors still must be finished after being laid. This involves four steps — sanding the surface, applying the first coat, sanding between coats, and applying the final coat.

1 **Wait until you're ready to** apply a finish before sanding the flooring. Don't sand it and let it sit for several weeks; it will get dirty. Rough sand the surface first, starting with 50-grit sandpaper and working up to 100-grit. Sand the main body of floor with a drum or an orbital sander, traveling with the grain. (You can rent these sanders from most tool rental services.) Sand small areas and edges with an edge sander or random orbit sander. Finish with 120-grit paper. (If you're finishing a parquet floor, work up to 180-grit.) **Note:** Wear a dust mask when you sand. Before you start, seal entrances to other rooms and put a fan in a window to exhaust air. This will keep the dust from creeping into other parts of the house.

2 **When applying the finish,** protect yourself and your family. Ventilate the room so finish fumes won't collect in the house, and wear a NIOSH/MSHA-approved respirator. Apply oil-base finishes with a bristle brush or short-nap roller, brushing with the grain to spread the finish out in a thin, even coat. Apply water-base finishes with a foam pad or short-nap roller so you don't apply too much at once. (If you flood a raw wood floor with a water-base finish, it will swell and distort.) **Note:** *Read the instructions* that come with the finish carefully.

(continued) ▷

FINISHING FLOORS — CONTINUED

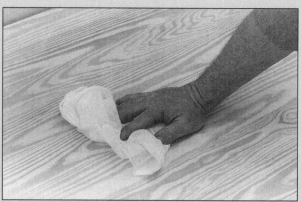

3 **Let the first coat dry as** recommended, then give it a light sanding with 240-grit or 320-grit sandpaper to knock down the high spots. If you have a floor buffer, it can be adapted to hold abrasive pads or *screenback* — an open-weave abrasive similar to drywall screen. Cut screenback discs the same size as the pads, rest the buffer on top of the disc, and turn it on. Go over the floor very lightly, keeping the buffer moving. You don't want to sand through the finish.

4 **Carefully vacuum the floor** and wipe up any dust that remains with a tack rag. Apply the second coat in the same manner as the first. Let it dry thoroughly (2 or 3 days) before walking on it. If you wish, wax and buff the floor to increase the gloss.

COMMON FLOOR FINISHES

TYPE	APPLICATION	COMMENTS
Polyurethane	Brush or roll on. Sand between coats.	Very durable but discolors in sunshine. Purchase a brand with a UV-inhibitor for sunny rooms. Relatively easy to apply and repair.
Water-borne finishes	Roll on. Finish is milky but dries clear. Sand between coats.	Fairly durable. Somewhat safer than solvent-based finishes. Very easy to apply and repair.
Oil finishes	Wipe on. Requires multiple coats. No need to sand between coats.	Not very durable. Won't protect against spills or abrasion. Extremely easy to apply and repair.
Acid-curing finishes	Add hardener, then brush or roll on. Sand between coats.	Extremely durable but highly toxic before they cure. Somewhat difficult to apply and repair. Also expensive.
Varnish	Brush on. Sand between coats.	Moderately durable. Fairly easy to apply and repair.
Shellac	Brush on. Sand between coats. Must be waxed or will spot.	Not very durable. Will not protect against spills. Produces very deep, warm finish. Easy to apply and repair.

5

WOOD WALL COVERINGS

I f you want some relief from the acres of monotonous plaster and drywall that cover the insides of most homes, wood is a warm and versatile alternative. It can be applied in a wide range of styles, from rustic planks to opulent frames and panels. You can attach the wood directly to the framing or apply it over other materials, cover an entire wall with it or just a portion.

The most commonly available wood wall coverings are sheet materials — veneer-covered plywood or hardboard. These are usually lumped together under the term *paneling.* There is also solid wood *plank paneling,* which fits together with rabbets or tongue-and-groove joints; *wainscoting,* which covers just the lower portion of a wall; and *framed paneling,* a frame-and-panel construction consisting of rails, stiles, and raised panels. Each requires a different method of installation.

Photo courtesy of Hyde Park Lumber Company, Cincinnati, Ohio

INSTALLING SHEET PANELING

Plywood and hardboard paneling are commonly available in several thicknesses, from ⅛ to ⅝ inch thick. The thickness you should use depends on the condition of the walls you intend to cover. If the walls are already covered with drywall or plaster and you plan to install the paneling over them, ⅛-inch-thick sheets are sufficient. You can use ¼-inch-thick panels if you cover bare studs with sheathing. However, paneling should be at least ⅜ inch thick if it will be attached directly to the framing.

If the walls are already covered, remove all moldings, casings, and trim. Find the studs and mark them by snapping chalk lines on the drywall or plaster. Each chalk line should indicate the center of a stud, as near as you can locate it. (SEE FIGURE 5-1.)

The seams between the paneling sheets must fall on the studs. To prevent the plaster or light-colored studs from showing through the seams of darker paneling, apply a dark paint or stain to the wall or the framing wherever the seams will fall. (SEE FIGURE 5-2.) Or simply trace the snap lines with a dark, wide-tipped indelible marker. This will prevent the seam from showing and it will still allow you to find the studs.

It's easier to begin (and end) the paneling at a corner. First cut the panel to length. Measure the distance between the floor and the ceiling and subtract ½ inch. When you install the panel, there should be a small gap between the top and the bottom to compensate for the unevenness of the floor and ceiling. (Moldings will hide these gaps.) Second, cut the panel to width. Because corners are not likely to be perfectly plumb or straight, you will have to trim the sheet to fit. Use a compass to transfer the corner's irregularities onto the edge of the panel, then cut it to shape. (SEE FIGURE 5-3.)

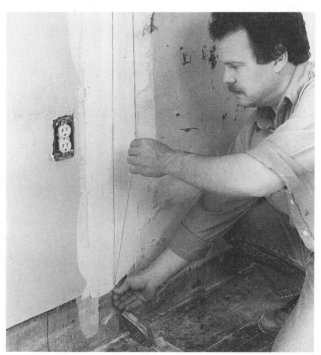

5-1 Clearly mark the locations of the studs *before* you install the first piece of paneling. Using a stud sensor, find the position of each stud near the floor *and* the ceiling. Drive a nail into the wall at each position to make sure you have found a stud. Stretch a snap line between the two nails and pluck it to put a chalk line on the wall — this line indicates the stud location.

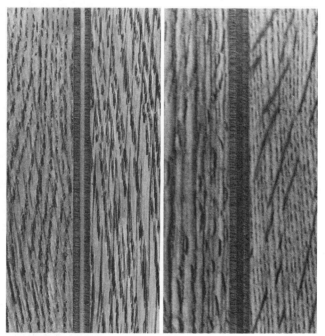

5-2 Although plywood and hardboard are relatively stable, they do shrink and swell slightly with changes in relative humidity. Consequently, the seams between the panels will open up slightly during dry weather. If the wood or the wall under these seams is a light color, it will show through the seams when the panels shrink. To make the seams less noticeable, paint or stain the material under them a dark color.

If you're hanging paneling over drywall, plaster, or builder's board, use both nails and construction adhesive. (The adhesive keeps the panels from buckling.) Apply beads of adhesive to the wall between the studs, then nail the panel to the studs. To attach the paneling directly to the studs, use nails only. (SEE FIGURE 5-4.) Leave a ¼-inch gap between the bottom of the panel and the floor. Set the panel on spacers as you nail it in place.

FOR BEST RESULTS

Use paneling nails to attach the paneling, and drive the nails through the dark seams wherever possible. Paneling nails are available in many different colors to match the paneling.

5-3 Begin installing the paneling in a corner. To fit the first sheet, measure from the corner to the center of the stud where you will join the second panel. Cut the first sheet 1 inch wider than needed, ripping the edge that fits the corner. Tack the sheet in place temporarily, with the edges plumb. Adjust a compass so the point is 1 inch from the scribe. Scribe the panel, tracing the irregularities in the corner with the compass point. Using a saber saw or a circular saw, cut the panel along the scribed line. Check that the sawed edge fits the corner and the other edge lays over the center of the stud.

5-4 If the wall is covered with drywall or plaster, apply beads of construction adhesive between the studs. Wait for the adhesive to flash (glaze over), then press the panel onto the wall. Set the panel on spacers to create a ¼-inch gap between the panel and the floor. Face nail the edges of the panel to the wall, driving the nails through the paneling and into the framing. Repeat, leaving a 1/16- to 1/8-inch-wide gap between each panel to allow for wood expansion. Without the gaps, the sheets may buckle.

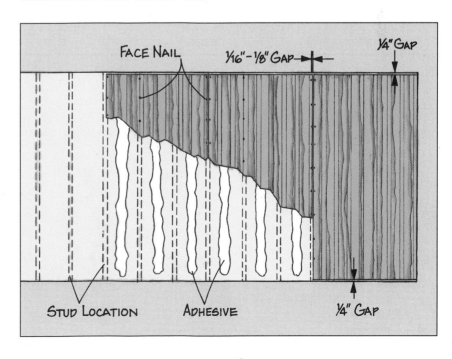

FACE NAIL   1/16"–1/8" GAP   ¼" GAP

STUD LOCATION   ADHESIVE   ¼" GAP

Working out from the corner, hang the remaining sheets in the same manner, nailing and gluing as necessary. Leave a 1/16- to 1/8-inch-wide gap between sheets to allow for expansion and contraction. As you work your way around the room, carefully measure door and window openings and the positions of electrical boxes. Mark the outlines of these features on the backs of the panels and cut openings for them with a saber saw or circular saw. (*SEE FIGURE 5-5.*) Check the fit of each panel and make sure the edges are plumb before fastening it to the wall.

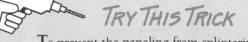

TRY THIS TRICK

To prevent the paneling from splintering or tearing out as you cut it, score the layout lines with an awl or a utility knife before you cut.

End the job the same way you began it — in a corner. Cover the inside and outside corners with trim. (*SEE FIGURE 5-6.*)

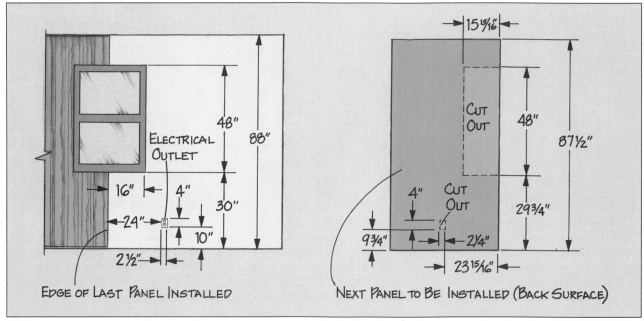

EDGE OF LAST PANEL INSTALLED

NEXT PANEL TO BE INSTALLED (BACK SURFACE)

5-5 To cut openings in the panels for doors, windows, and electrical boxes, measure the horizontal and vertical position of each item. Use the edge of the last panel installed as a reference point for the horizontal measurements, and the floor as the reference for vertical measurements. Transfer these measurements to the *back* of the panel you will next install. As you do so, subtract 1/16 inch from the horizontal measurements to compensate for the gap between panels and 1/4 inch from the vertical measurements for the gap between the panel and the floor. Cut the openings with a saber saw or circular saw, then check to see if the panel fits.

5-6 To hide the rough edges and the plies on sheet materials, you must cover the corners with molding. *Quarter-rounds* and small *coves* (1) are used to hide inside corners, while *corner guards* (2) cover outside corners. To fasten the moldings to the paneling, face nail them with small finishing nails.

INSTALLING PLANK PANELING AND WAINSCOTING

Before plywood and hardboard became popular, the most common type of paneling was narrow strips of solid wood which fit together with overlapping rabbets or tongue-and-groove joints. You can still purchase solid wood paneling, although it's a great deal more expensive than sheet materials. Plank paneling comes in long strips that run from the floor to the ceiling, while wainscoting comes in shorter lengths, running partway up a wall.

How you apply these materials depends on how thick they are. If they are ½ inch thick or thicker, you can simply nail them to the wall. Thinner planks and wainscoting should be attached with nails *and* mastic.

The nails must be anchored in horizontal framing members or grounding, unless the manufacturer's directions say otherwise. This often means you must install grounding partway up the walls to anchor the middle of the plank paneling or the top of the wain-

scoting. If the walls are already covered, this can present a problem. You could nail grounding strips over the plaster or drywall, but this would make the walls unnecessarily thick (and the room smaller). Instead, remove a narrow band of the plaster or drywall and attach the grounding directly to the studs. (*SEE FIGURE 5-7.*)

If you're installing plank paneling, cut all the strips about ¼ inch shorter than the distance between the floor and the ceiling. If you're installing wainscoting, snap a horizontal line around the perimeter of the room to mark the top of the wainscoting. Cut the strips about ¼ inch shorter than the distance between the floor and the line.

As with sheet materials, the best place to start installing plank paneling is a corner. Join the first two pieces together in the corner with the tongues facing in the direction you will be proceeding. (*SEE FIGURE 5-8.*) Make

5-7 To anchor the middle of paneling planks or the top of wainscoting, install one-by-four grounding partway up the wall. If the walls are already covered with plaster or drywall, cut away a horizontal band of this material about 6 inches wide all around the room. Notch the exposed studs and fasten the grounding to them so the strips are flush with the walls. **Note:** If you are installing wainscoting, position the grounding several inches below where the top edge of the wainscoting will rest. When the wainscoting is fastened to the wall, it should hide the area where you removed the wall covering.

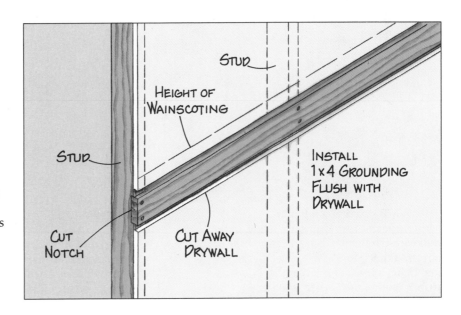

5-8 There are two ways to join plank paneling and wainscoting in an inside corner. Butt the arrises together, leaving an open space at the corner (1), or butt the edge of one strip against the face of the other (2). Likewise, there are two ways to join the strips at an outside corner. Butt an edge against a face (3), or miter the edges (4).

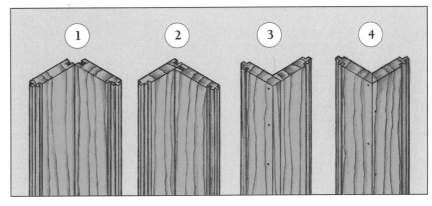

sure the first pieces are plumb. If necessary, scribe the edge of one corner piece to fit it to the other. (SEE FIGURE 5-9.)

As you work your way around the room, fit the grooves to the tongues, then blind nail through the tongues. Or, if the tongues are too thin to blind nail, apply adhesive to the wall, wait for it to flash, and face nail the strips. (SEE FIGURE 5-10.) Check that the

strips remain plumb as the job progresses. When you reach an inside corner, rip a piece to fit the remaining space and face nail it to the wall. To turn an outside corner, join two strips at right angles to fit over the corner like a cap. If you find a corner is out of plumb, taper a piece to fit it. (SEE FIGURE 5-11.) Plan the work so you can end the same way you began — in a corner.

5-9 When starting a job in a corner, attach the first strip to one wall with the tongue facing in the direction that you will be proceeding. Using a level, check that the strip is plumb, then fasten it to the wall by face nailing near the edge that's in the corner and blind nailing through the tongue. Snap a plumb line on the adjacent wall, about 1 inch out from the corner. Temporarily tack a strip to the wall so the grooved edge is even with the plumb line. Measure the gap between the grooved edge and the first strip. Adjust a compass so the distance between the point and the scribe is equal to the widest part of the gap and scribe the second strip. Saw or plane the strip to the scribe marks, fit it against the first strip, and nail it to the wall.

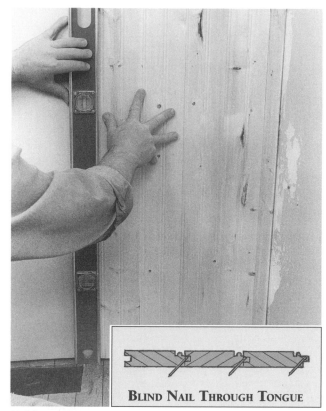

BLIND NAIL THROUGH TONGUE

5-10 Cut all paneling planks ½ inch shorter than the space between the floor and ceiling. Make wainscoting ¼ inch shorter than the space you have to fill. If you're installing plank paneling, rest it on ¼-inch spacers as you put it up. This will create a small gap between the floor and ceiling. If you're installing wainscoting, position the tops even with the horizontal line you snapped on the walls. There will be a ¼-inch-wide gap between the bottoms of the strips and the floor. All gaps will be covered later by molding. Also, check with a level to make sure each strip is plumb. When you're sure it's positioned correctly, fasten it to the wall with nails.

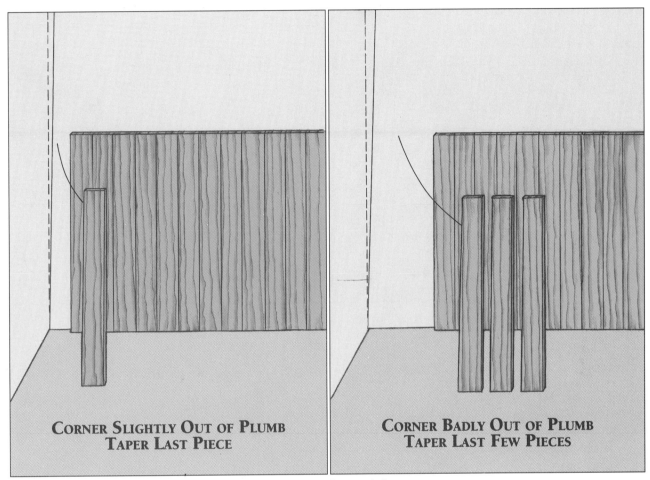

**CORNER SLIGHTLY OUT OF PLUMB
TAPER LAST PIECE**

**CORNER BADLY OUT OF PLUMB
TAPER LAST FEW PIECES**

5-11 When you come to a corner that's slightly out of plumb, cut a matching taper in the strip that butts up to the corner. If the corner is badly out of plumb, cut a slight taper in the last three or four strips before the corner. This will spread the change in vertical alignment over several pieces and the irregular corner won't be as noticeable as it might have been.

INSTALLING FRAMES AND PANELS

Framed paneling consists of vertical *stiles,* horizontal *rails,* and raised *panels.* You can purchase ready-to-install systems with solid wood rails and stiles and veneered panels, or you can make your own. *(SEE FIGURE 5-12.)* Either option is likely to be expensive, but the opulent appearance of a classic frame-and-panel wall is well worth the price. *(SEE FIGURE 5-13.)*

As with plank paneling and wainscoting, framed paneling requires grounding midway up the wall to properly anchor the stiles. Install the grounding as shown in *FIGURE 5-7* on page 61, then measure and mark the locations of the stiles. *(SEE FIGURE 5-14.)* Adjust the length of the rails, if necessary. Start the job at a corner, face nailing two adjacent stiles (one on each wall).

Join the rails to one of the corner stiles. If you are installing a classic system with grooved frame members, slide the panels into the grooves, then attach the next stile to the rails. Face nail the stile to the wall and repeat. If you are installing a contemporary system, simply join the rails and stiles, nailing the stiles in place as you go. When all the frame members are installed, cut moldings to fit inside the frame openings. Place each panel in its opening and attach the moldings around the perimeter of the opening to keep the panel in place.

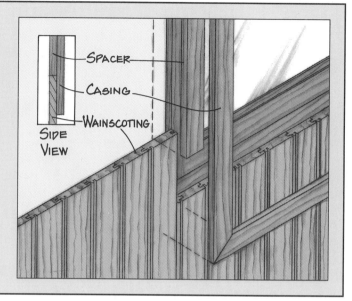

For Your Information

If you plan to reinstall old trim in a room after you panel it, you'll have to add spacers and extension jambs behind the door and window casings. These spacers must be equal to the thickness of the paneling.

SPACER

CASING

WAINSCOTING

SIDE VIEW

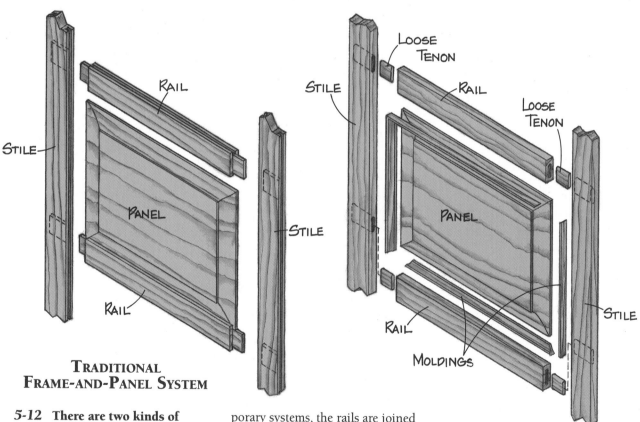

RAIL

STILE

STILE

PANEL

RAIL

TRADITIONAL FRAME-AND-PANEL SYSTEM

LOOSE TENON

STILE

RAIL

LOOSE TENON

PANEL

STILE

RAIL

MOLDINGS

CONTEMPORARY FRAME-AND-PANEL SYSTEM

5-12 There are two kinds of framed-panel systems, each installed in a slightly different manner. In a classic system, the rails and stiles are joined with mortises and tenons. The inside edges of the frame members are grooved, and the raised panels rest in the grooves. In some contem-porary systems, the rails are joined with dowels or loose tenons. The panels are held in place with mold-ings around the inside edges of the frame members. Because of the dowels and moldings, there are more pieces in a contemporary system, but they are easier to install.

5-13 Both framed-panel systems look similar when installed. This finished contemporary system is almost indistinguishable from a classic one. *Photo courtesy of Hyde Park Lumber Company, Cincinnati, Ohio.*

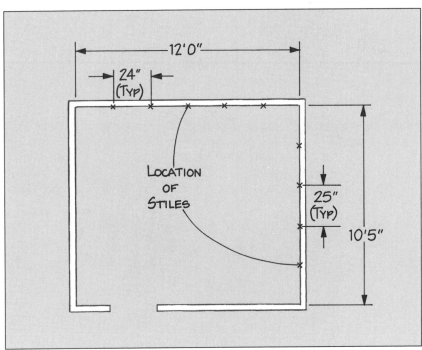

5-14 You must plan the frames and panels so the stiles are spaced evenly and meet at the corners. To do this, you'll have to adjust the length of the rails accordingly. The rails are often slightly different lengths on each wall.

6

CASINGS, MOLDINGS, AND TRIM

The finishing touch on any finish carpentry job is the trim. *Casings* frame doors and windows; *moldings* delineate the transitions between floors, walls, and ceilings, adding visual interest to a room; and other *trim* disguises rough cuts and open joints that are often necessary when building a home. For example, a window casing covers the rough edges in the wall covering where the window opening was cut. A baseboard molding covers the small gap that a drywall hanger leaves between the drywall and the floor.

Trim work is also an excellent opportunity for some creative craftsmanship. When installing doors, windows, floors, and wall coverings, most carpenters work with ready-made materials that are designed and crafted elsewhere. But moldings and casings are also easy to make yourself with a router and a table saw. And even if you purchase manufactured trim, you can mix and match the shapes to create a unique architectural effect.

TRIMMING DOORS AND WINDOWS

The trim that surrounds a window or door is called a *casing* (or casement). This casing frames the opening and covers the joints between the wall covering and the jamb. It's available in dozens of different profiles, from simple rectangles to intricately molded shapes. (*SEE FIGURE 6-1.*)

INSTALLING DOOR CASINGS

Not only is there a wide selection of casing shapes, you can arrange the casing around an opening in several different ways. For example, when installing a door casing, you can butt the strips together, miter them, or join them with rectangular pieces called *plinths* and *corner blocks*. Use a single casing shape, or mix different shapes. (*SEE FIGURE 6-2.*)

Before you install a casing, decide where the casing will meet the jamb. Normally, the casing is installed so part of the jamb edge shows. The portion of the edge that's exposed is called the *reveal*. Mark the reveal on the jambs, then carefully measure the *reveal opening* — this is what you must frame with the casing. (*SEE FIGURE 6-3.*)

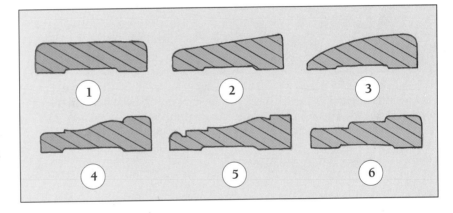

6-1 Casing is available in dozens of different shapes. Shown are six common profiles — *roundover* (1), *face* (2), *thumbnail* (3), *ogee* (4), *ogee-and-bead* (5), and *three-step* (6). Most commercial casing is between $9/16$ and $11/16$ inch thick and $2^1/4$ to $3^1/2$ inches wide. It usually has a slight recess in the back surface so the casing will lay flat even if it cups slightly.

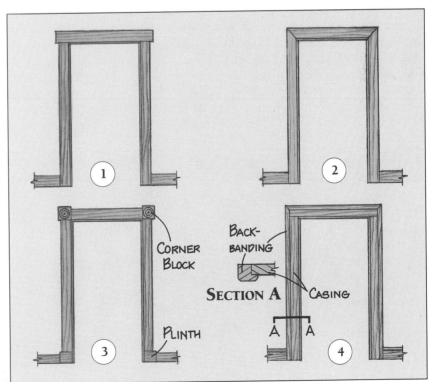

6-2 There are several ways to join the parts of a door casing. Shown are four common methods — *butted* (1), *mitered* (2), *butted* with *plinths* and *corner blocks* (3), and *butted* with *mitered backbanding* (4).

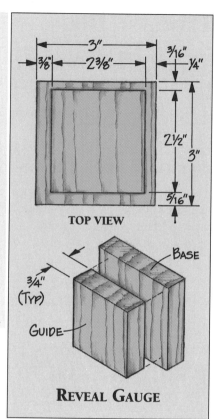

TOP VIEW

REVEAL GAUGE

BASE

GUIDE

3/4"
(TYP)

6-3 Normally, the casing is attached to the jamb so part of the jamb edge shows. The visible portion is called the *reveal*. It's the reveal opening you must frame, not the jamb opening. However, before you can fit the casing to the reveal, you must mark it. Scribe lines on the edge of the jamb, typically 3/16 to 3/8 inch from the inside surface. The jig shown helps mark a consistent reveal.

Also consider the floor covering. If you plan to install new carpeting or flooring, the vertical casing members should be cut short so the new material will fit under them. **Note:** For most carpeting, the bottom ends of the casing should be 1/4 inch above the floor. For other flooring, measure the thickness of the material and subtract this from the length of the vertical members.

Cut the casing parts to frame the reveal, fitting each part as you go. As a rule of thumb, it's easier to start at the bottom and work up. Cut the vertical parts of the casing first, then the horizontal (top) piece. If you're butting the parts of the casing together, don't presume that you can make all cuts at 90 degrees. Oftentimes, you must allow for floors that aren't quite level and jambs that aren't quite square. (*SEE FIGURES 6-4 THROUGH 6-6.*) The same considerations apply when the casings are mitered — you will have to adjust the angle for some joints. (*SEE FIGURES 6-7 AND 6-8.*)

 FOR BEST RESULTS

In addition to off-level floors and out-of-square jambs, you may find that the walls are not perfectly flat and the casing parts are slightly warped. When this happens, the faces of the members won't meet at the same level — one will be higher than the other. If the levels are only slightly different, you can sand or plane the members flush. When the levels are badly mismatched, insert shims behind the low member. If this creates a visible gap between the casing and the wall, cut a strip of wood to fill it.

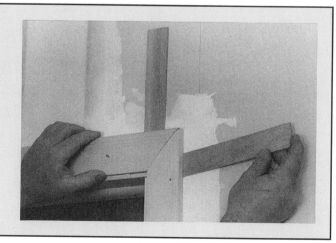

6-4 Unless you're planning to install carpeting or some other floor covering later, fit the side casings to the floor. Clamp or tack each casing in place on the jamb, aligning the inside edge with the reveal mark. Adjust a compass so there's a fraction of an inch between the point and the scribe, then scribe the casing near the bottom end. Cut the casing along this mark.

6-5 Once you've cut the bottom ends of the side casings, tack them in place. Mark the inside edges where they meet the top reveal line. Hold the top casing piece across the side casings. Align the bottom edge with the reveal marks and, using the top piece like a straightedge, scribe lines across the side casings. Cut the casings to length along these marks.

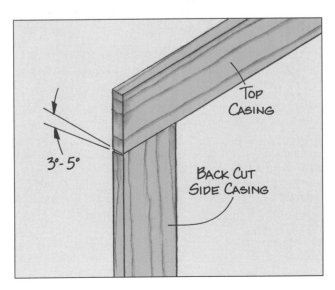

6-6 Oftentimes, you can get a better fit on a butt joint if you *back-cut* the butt end. Cut through the thickness 3 to 5 degrees off square, as shown. Arrange the molding so the outside arris butts against the adjacent casing member.

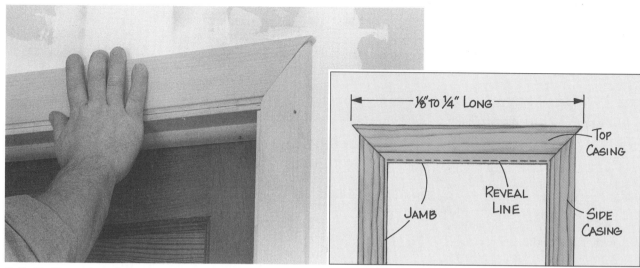

6-7 To fit a mitered door casing, miter all the parts at 45 degrees, but cut the *top* piece ⅛ to ¼ inch long. Tack the vertical pieces in place. Rest the top piece on them and position it so the bottom edge is parallel with the reveal line. Inspect the miter joints. If they're tight, cut the piece to the proper length, mitering the ends at 45 degrees. If there's a gap in the joints, adjust the miter angles accordingly when you cut the pieces to length.

6-8 Sometimes all that's needed to fit a miter joint is to adjust the miter angle a fraction of a degree. When this is the case, use a *shooting board* and a hand plane to trim or *shoot* the mitered end. Adjust the back stop to the proper angle or insert a shim between the stop and the casing to achieve the necessary angle. A shooting board is a handy jig for trimming butt joints, too. (For plans and instructions on how to make a shooting board, see the "Shooting Board/Miter Box" on page 73.)

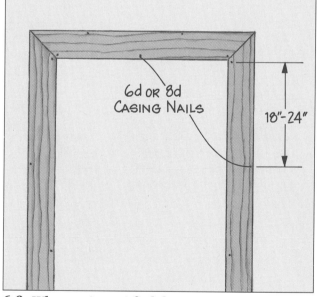

6-9 When you're satisfied that the parts of the casing fit well, drive casing nails through the casing and into both the jamb and the framing around the jamb. (Use 6d nails for casing up to ¾ inch thick and 8d nails for thicker stock.) Space the nails 18 to 24 inches apart and stagger them, driving one into a jamb and the next into the framing. Set the nail heads slightly below the casing surface.

As you cut the parts and fit the joints, tack the members to the wall, but don't drive the nails all the way home. The casing shouldn't be fastened permanently until all the parts fit to your satisfaction. (SEE FIGURES 6-9 AND 6-10.)

6-10 **If the casings are mitered,** *lock nail* the corners to keep them from pulling apart. Drive the first nail through the edge of one piece and into the end of the other. Drive the second nail 90 degrees from the first.

INSTALLING WINDOW CASINGS

Most window casings are installed with a shelf or a *stool* at the bottom and an *apron* under the stool. The sides and top of the casing can be butted, mitered, or joined with blocks. But in some newer homes, window casings have no stools; they are installed like a picture frame. (SEE FIGURE 6-11.)

Window casings are installed in much the same manner as door casings. Mark the reveal on the jambs and measure the reveal opening. Begin at the bottom of the casing — if it includes a stool, start with that. Measure and mark the *horns*, the parts of the stool that extend past the side jambs. Cut the horns and install the stool. (SEE FIGURE 6-12.)

Add the vertical pieces, followed by the top and the apron, in that order. If necessary, scribe and trim the ends of the vertical casings to fit off-level stools or top pieces, then miter and *return* the ends of the apron. (SEE FIGURES 6-13 AND 6-14.) Tack all the parts in place. When you're satisfied with the fit, drive the nails home and set the heads.

6-11 **There are several ways to** join the parts of a window casing. Shown are five of the most common arrangements — *picture frame* (1), *stool-and-apron* with a *butted top* (2), *stool-and-apron* with a *mitered top* (3), *stool-and-apron* with *corner blocks* (4), and *stool-and-apron* with a *cabinet head* (5).

6-12 **When installing trim on a**
window, begin with the *stool,* if there
is one. This stool fills the space inside
the jambs, creating a shelf. Narrow
horns extend past the outside edges
of the side casing. Mark the horns on
the stool so they are equal in length.
Cut the horns with a coping saw or
saber saw, then attach the stool to
the sill with finishing nails.

6-13 **Cut and attach the side**
casings and the top casing in the
same manner as a door casing. Fit
each part, compensating for jambs
that aren't quite plumb or square.

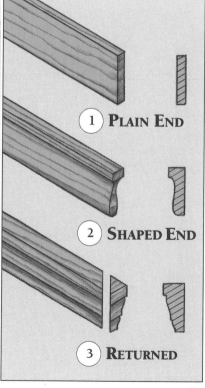

1. **PLAIN END**

2. **SHAPED END**

3. **RETURNED**

6-14 **Last of all, attach the *apron***
under the stool. If the apron is a
simple rectangle, you can leave the
ends plain (1). But if it's molded, you
may wish to *shape* the ends (2) to
match the molding. Or, miter the ends
and *return* them (3). Both options
will give the apron a finished look.

TRY THIS TRICK

Instead of hiding the nail heads with putty, use a blind nail plane. This special plane raises a small curl of wood without actually separating it from the board. Drive the nail through the depression where the curl was cut, set the head, and glue the curl back in place. After a light sanding, you won't be able to tell that you even used nails.

SHOOTING BOARD/MITER BOX

Sometimes, all you need to do to fit a butt joint or a miter is adjust the angle just a little bit. When this is the case, you can do the job with a *shooting board* and a hand plane a lot faster than you can with a saw. This particular shooting board has an

adjustable backstop, so you can easily set it to shoot the angle needed. The backstop is actually a hardwood miter box — you can build your own or use a commercially made box. This enables you to cut the miters and shoot them with the same fixture.

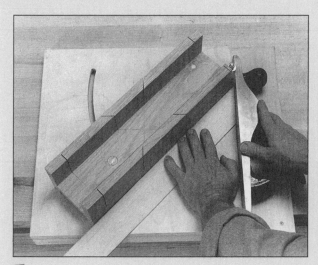

1 **To shoot a butt joint or a** miter, adjust the miter box/back stop to the proper angle. Place the molding against the stop and position it so the end protrudes ever so slightly past the edge of the guide. Turn a bench plane on its side, hold the bottom against the guide, and shave the end of the molding until you've changed the angle.

2 **To use the miter box, place** the stock between the hardwood sides and cut it with a back saw, using the slots in the sides to guide the saw. You don't have to change the shooting angle to do this, so you can cut a miter and trim without having to change the setup each time.

(continued) ▷

SHOOTING BOARD/MITER BOX — CONTINUED

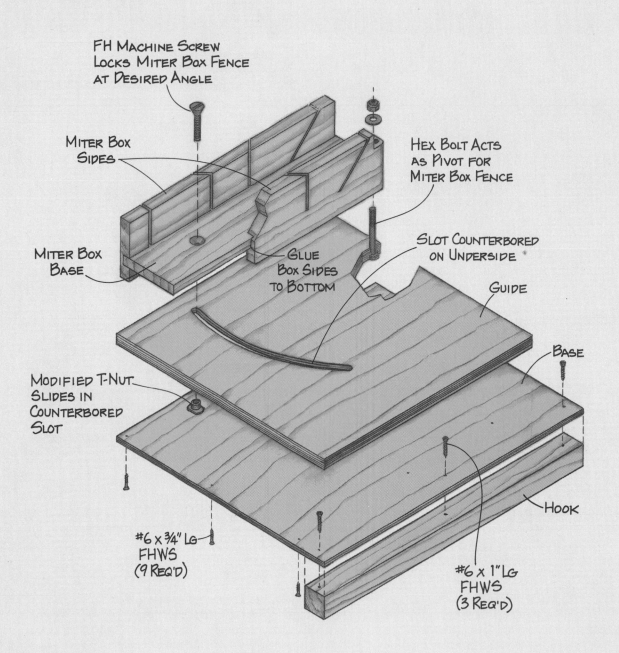

FH MACHINE SCREW
LOCKS MITER BOX FENCE
AT DESIRED ANGLE

MITER BOX
SIDES

MITER BOX
BASE

HEX BOLT ACTS
AS PIVOT FOR
MITER BOX FENCE

GLUE
BOX SIDES
TO BOTTOM

SLOT COUNTERBORED
ON UNDERSIDE

GUIDE

BASE

MODIFIED T-NUT
SLIDES IN
COUNTERBORED
SLOT

#6 X ¾" LG
FHWS
(9 REQ'D)

#6 X 1" LG
FHWS
(3 REQ'D)

HOOK

EXPLODED VIEW

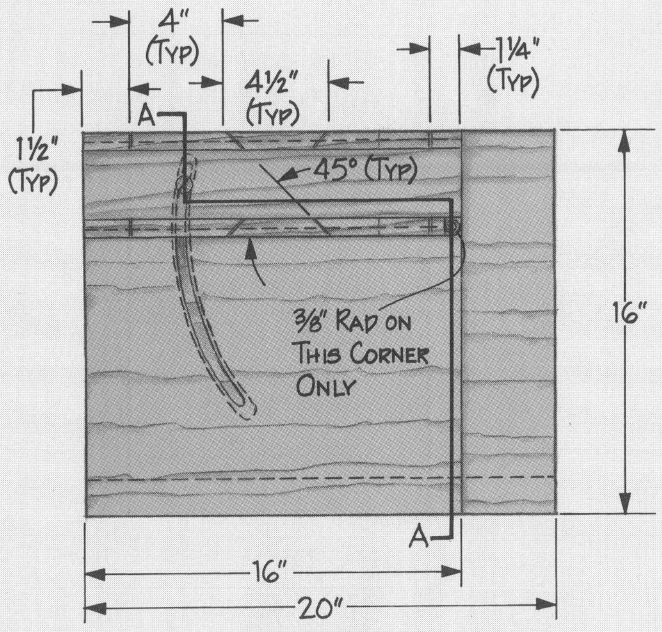
4" (Typ)
4½" (Typ)
1¼" (Typ)
1½" (Typ)
A
45° (Typ)
3/8" Rad on This Corner Only
16"
16"
20"
A

Top View

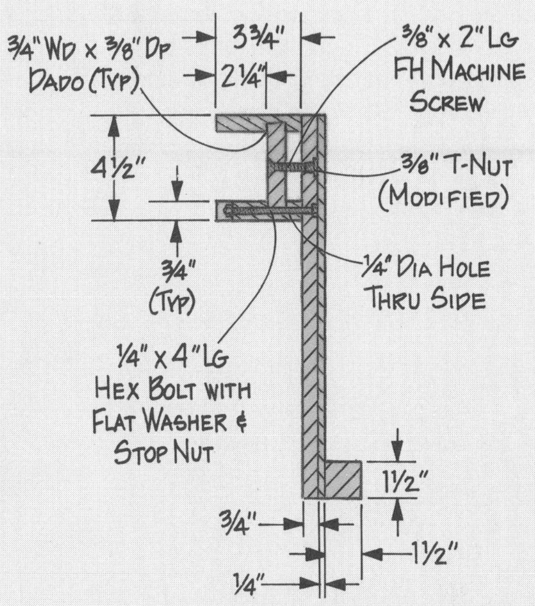
3/4" Wd x 3/8" Dp Dado (Typ)
3¾"
2¼"
3/8" x 2" Lg FH Machine Screw
4½"
3/8" T-Nut (Modified)
3/4" (Typ)
1/4" Dia Hole Thru Side
1/4" x 4" Lg Hex Bolt with Flat Washer & Stop Nut
1½"
3/4"
1½"
1/4"

Section A

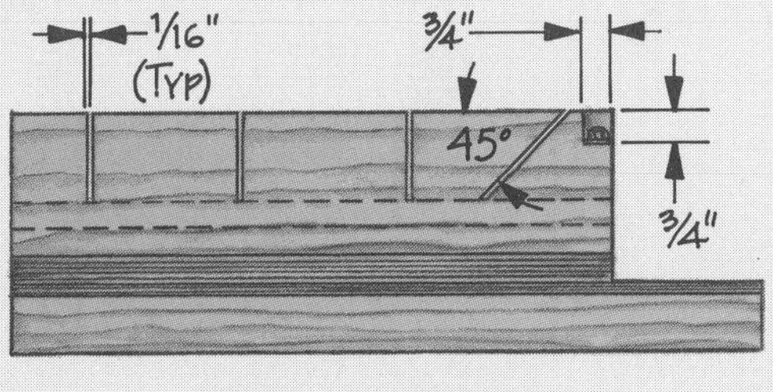
1/16" (Typ)
3/4"
45°
3/4"

Front View

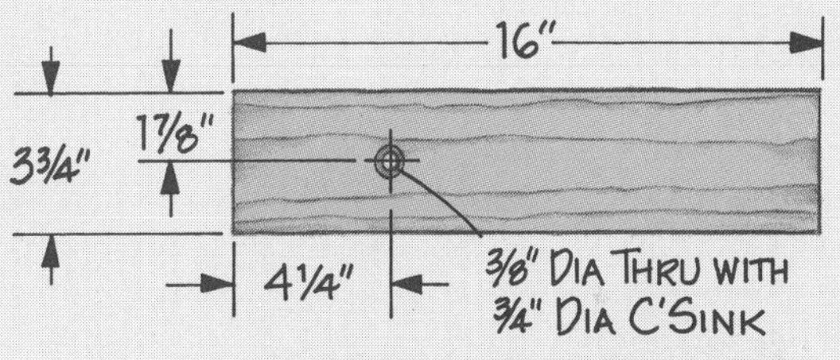
16"
3¾"
1⅞"
4¼"
3/8" Dia Thru with 3/4" Dia C'Sink

Miter Box Base Layout

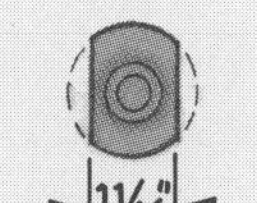
11/16"

TOP VIEW

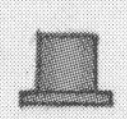

SIDE VIEW

T-Nut Modifications

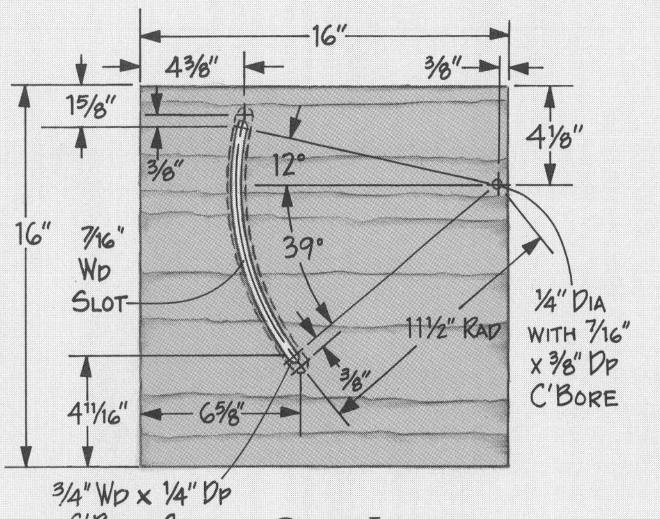
16"
4⅜"
3/8"
1⅝"
4⅛"
3/8"
12°
16"
7/16" Wd Slot
39°
11½" Rad
1/4" Dia with 7/16" x 3/8" Dp C'Bore
3/8"
4 11/16"
6⅝"
3/4" Wd x 1/4" Dp C'Bore Slot

Guide Layout

TRIMMING FLOORS, WALLS, AND CEILINGS

Once you have framed the doors and windows in a room, you might also trim the floors, walls, and ceilings. *Baseboards* disguise the joints between the floors and walls; *chair rails* and *picture rails* add visual interest; *ceiling moldings* can make the ceiling appear higher or lower. All of these moldings help to tie the architectural elements in the room together.

Some moldings are just one piece; others are built up from several pieces. *(SEE FIGURE 6-15.)* Additionally, there are many profiles for each piece. *(SEE FIGURE 6-16.)* You can mix and match these to make an almost endless variety of styles and effects. A traditional cornice, for example, is made from several different moldings.

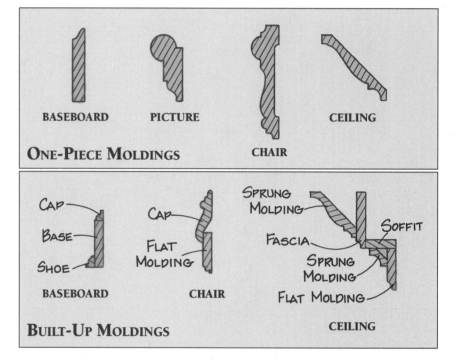

6-15 Trim can be plain or fancy, one piece or many. You can install one-piece baseboards, chair rails, and ceiling moldings, or you can build them up from several pieces. Baseboards are often built from *base, cap* and *shoe* moldings. Chair rails can be assembled from *flat* and *cap* moldings. Ceiling moldings (or cornices) sometimes consist of *sprung, fascia, soffit,* and *flat* moldings.

6-16 There are many different shapes available that you can mix and match when building up trim. Shown are just a few of the more common base, shoe, cap, flat, and sprung moldings. **Note:** When assembling ceiling moldings, flat moldings also serve as soffits and fascia.

INSTALLING BASEBOARDS, CHAIR RAILS, AND PICTURE RAILS

Like casings, baseboards and other horizontal moldings are cut to fit, then installed with finishing nails. When fitting the moldings, there are a few important rules of thumb:

- Miter outside corners.
- Cope inside corners.
- Butt baseboards and chair rails to casings.

Mitering an outside corner is a straightforward operation — put the baseboard in position, mark it, and cut it. However, you may have to adjust the angle if the corner isn't plumb or the floor isn't level. To do this, make the first cut a little wide and check that the saw cut is parallel with the mark. If it isn't, change the angle accordingly. (SEE FIGURE 6-17.)

When coping an inside corner, you must cut the end of one piece to fit the face of the other. To do this, butt the first piece of baseboard into the corner. Cut the second piece as if you were making a miter joint. Cut the shape of the cope, following the arris between the mitered end and the molded face. Fit the coped end against the face of the first piece. (SEE FIGURES 6-18 AND 6-19.)

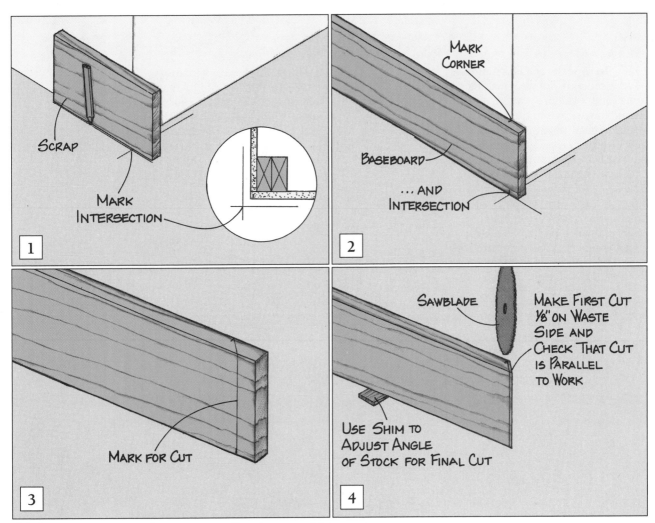

6-17 To miter an outside corner on a baseboard, use a scrap to mark the floor where the outside surfaces will meet. Hold the baseboard in place and mark the inside of the miter at the corner of the wall. Mark the outside where the marks on the floor intersect. Make a miter cut about 1/8 inch wide of the mark to see if the saw will pass through both. If it won't, eyeball the correct angle, then either adjust the chop saw or use a shim to reposition the molding.

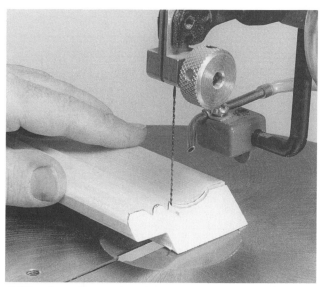

6-18 To cope the end of a molding,
cut the end as if you were making a
miter joint. (The point of the miter
should fit snugly in the corner.)
Using a pencil, shade the arris
between the mitered end and the
molded face. Clamp the molding to a
bench, with the flat surface that will
fit against the wall facing *down.* Saw
along the arris with a coping saw,
holding the blade plumb. **Note:**
Many craftsmen prefer to back-cut
coped joints. This will eliminate any
gaps if the wall isn't perfectly flat or
the molding is slightly warped.

6-19 If you have a benchtop
scroll saw that you can carry to the
job site, you can use it to make coped
joints. Fit the saw with a *spiral blade*
(one that cuts in all directions).
This will enable you to cut the cope
without turning the molding. If you
want to back-cut, tilt the table 3 to 5
degrees.

 FOR YOUR INFORMATION

If you wish to use *corner blocks,* as shown in this
Victorian baseboard, you can get by without mitering
or coping the base molding at all. Most of the joints
are butted; only the shoe molding is mitered.

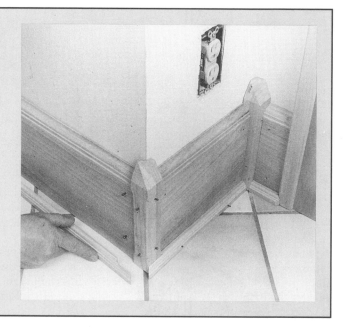

To butt a molding to a casing, cut the end to fit against it snugly. Once again, a simple 90-degree cut will not work if the casement is not plumb. Mark the molding in place, then cut it to fit. (SEE FIGURE 6-20.)

Here are a few additional techniques that come in handy from time to time:

■ If the floor is extremely uneven, scribe the bottom edge of the baseboard and fit it to the floor. (SEE FIGURE 6-21.)

■ Join two or more short pieces with scarf joints to make a long molding. (SEE FIGURE 6-22.)

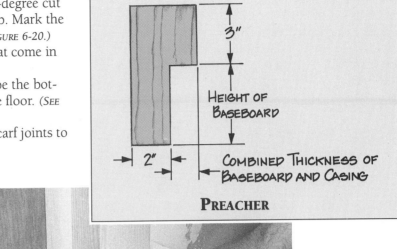

3"

HEIGHT OF BASEBOARD

2"

COMBINED THICKNESS OF BASEBOARD AND CASING

PREACHER

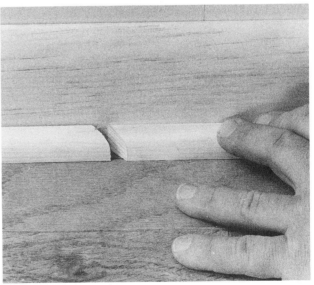

6-20   To cut a baseboard to fit snugly against a casing, use a *preacher* to mark it. This simple jig copies the proper angle for the cut. Put the baseboard in position on the wall and hold it against the casing. Put the preacher over the baseboard and press it against the outside edge of the casing. Using a mouse (a carpenter's pencil halved lengthwise), mark the baseboard where the preacher straddles it. Cut along this mark.

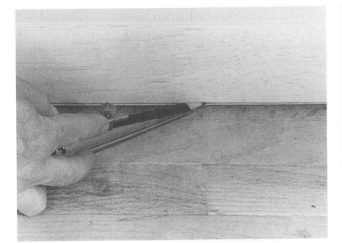

6-21   If the floor is uneven, you may have to cut the baseboard to fit it. Place the baseboard in position and measure the widest gap between the bottom edge and the floor. Adjust a compass so the distance between the point and the scribe is equal to the widest gap. Scribe the baseboard with the compass, then cut or plane the bottom edge to the scribed line.

6-22   When you must join pieces to make one long molding, cut *scarf joints.* Miter the adjacent ends of the molding pieces at 45 degrees so they overlap. Try to match the wood grain and the color of the pieces as closely as possible.

■ Should you need to end a molding, cut a bevel or a miter in the end, shape the end, or return the molding. (SEE FIGURE 6-23.)

■ Fasten baseboards and caps to the wall, but nail shoes to the floor. If the baseboards should shrink, the shoes will hide the gap between the baseboard and the floor.

TRY THIS TRICK

When fastening small, thin moldings, such as the shoes on a baseboard, *spin* the finishing nails partway in. This prevents the nails from splitting the molding. Chuck each nail head in a cordless drill, turn on the drill, and drive the nail into the molding as far as you can. Loosen the chuck and drive the nail the rest of the way with a hammer.

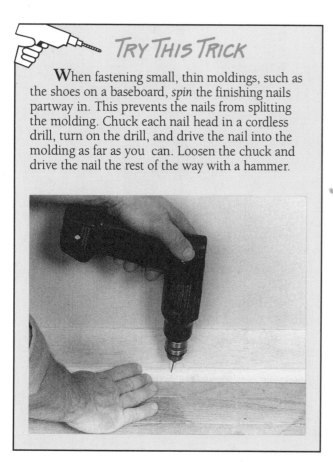

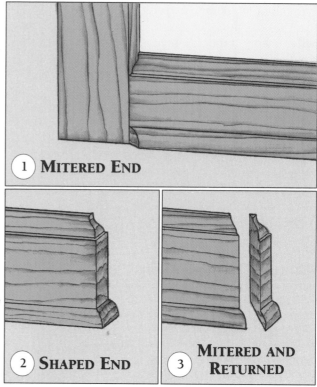

1 MITERED END

2 SHAPED END

3 MITERED AND RETURNED

6-23 Moldings usually run in a continuous ring around a room or butt against casings. However, sometimes you must end a molding. For instance, shoe moldings often end at a door opening because they protrude beyond the casing. To give the shoe a finished look, craftsmen usually *miter* the end (1). If the molding is large and more complex, you can *shape* the end (2), or miter and *return* it (3).

INSTALLING CEILING MOLDINGS

Most ceiling moldings are fitted and installed in much the same way as other horizontal moldings — miter the outside corners, cope the inside corners, and fasten the molding in place with finishing nails. However, when the ceiling trim includes sprung moldings — crown, bed, or cove — there are two additional considerations.

First, sprung moldings may require additional grounding because they are *sloped* — set at an angle to the wall rather than fastened flat against it. A single horizontal strip in the wall may not provide a sufficient anchor. Depending on how the ceiling molding is built up, you may have to attach grounding strips to the ceiling *and* the wall. (SEE FIGURE 6-24.)

Second, crown, bed, and cove moldings are mitered and coped in a slightly different manner than moldings that lie flat on the wall. Using a chop saw or miter box, hold them at the proper slope and with the top edge down. (SEE FIGURE 6-25.) If the sprung molding is too tall to cut in this manner, you'll have to lay it flat and cut a *compound miter* — tilt the blade and adjust the miter angle. To determine the angles needed to set up for a compound miter, first determine the slope of the molding — measure its angle from the wall and subtract this from 90 degrees. Then use these two formulas:

Blade tilt = *sine* (slope) x 45°
Miter angle = 90° - [*cosine* (slope) x 45°]

For example, if the slope of the molding is 45 degrees, tilt the blade at 31½ degrees and set the miter angle at 58 degrees to cut a compound miter. **Note:** Any scientific calculator will figure sines and cosines for you, or you can look them up in an algebra or trigonometry text.

When coping a sprung molding, rotate the molding 90 degrees so the top and bottom edges face sideways. Look straight down on the molding as you cut it with the coping saw. (*SEE FIGURES 6-26 AND 6-27.*)

When you have installed all the trim, cover the nail heads and caulk any gaps. If you plan to paint the

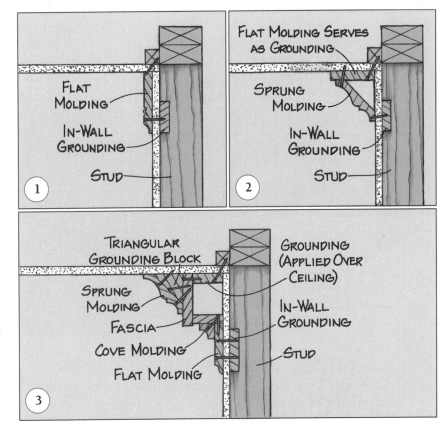

6-24 Ceiling moldings sometimes require more grounding than other types, especially when they incorporate sprung moldings. A simple flat ceiling molding can be anchored to the top plate or a single grounding strip (1), but a crown molding may require two strips — one in the wall and another on the ceiling (2). Complex ceiling moldings, such as a formal cornice with a fascia and a soffit (3), need additional anchors.

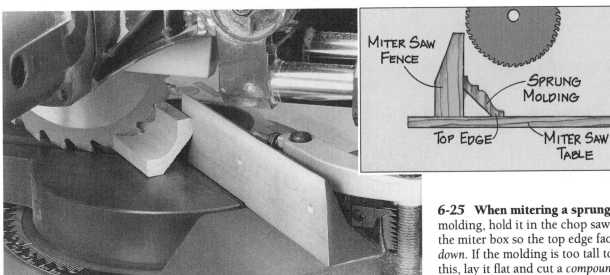

6-25 When mitering a sprung molding, hold it in the chop saw or the miter box so the top edge faces *down*. If the molding is too tall to do this, lay it flat and cut a *compound miter.*

trim, automotive body putty makes an excellent filler since it dries quickly and sands easily. If the trim will be stained and finished, make a filler by mixing water putty with a water-based aniline dye that matches the stain you will use. The putty will dry very light, but it will darken when you apply the finish. If you use the same dye to stain the trim, the filler will be almost indistinguishable from the finished moldings.

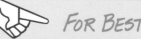

FOR BEST RESULTS

Many craftsmen prefer to finish trim *before* they install it permanently. First, fit the trim, tacking it in place temporarily; then remove it and apply a finish. After the finish dries, install it permanently. Set the nail heads and touch up the finish around them. This is easier than finishing molding in place and helps prevent you from spilling finish on walls and floors.

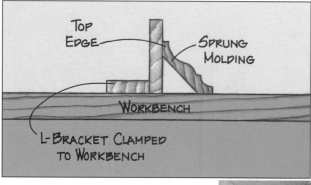

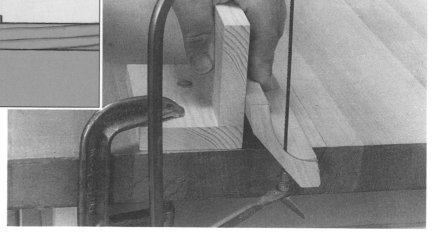

6-26 To cope a sprung molding, miter it as described in *FIGURE 6-25*. Then hold it as shown here and cut along the arris between the mitered end and the molded face. Hold the coping saw straight up and down.

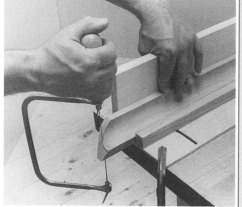

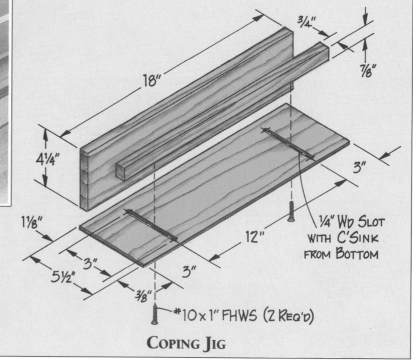

6-27 To help hold a sprung molding while you cut a miter or a cope, make this simple jig. Place the edge of the molding against the stop and adjust the position of the stop to hold the molding at the proper slope.

COPING JIG

PROJECTS

7

COFFERED CEILING

One of the most elegant ways to trim a ceiling is to put up *coffering,* a gridwork of moldings that divides the ceiling into deep, recessed panels. And while the effect is grand, it's not difficult to do. You can make a coffered ceiling using ordinary techniques for installing trim.

Although coffering looks like it's made from solid beams, the beams are hollow, U-shaped channels made from flat moldings. These channels are held to the ceiling by *grounding* — strips of wood attached with molly anchors and lag screws. The moldings that make up the coffering are joined like most horizontal trim. The outside corners are mitered, and the inside corners are coped.

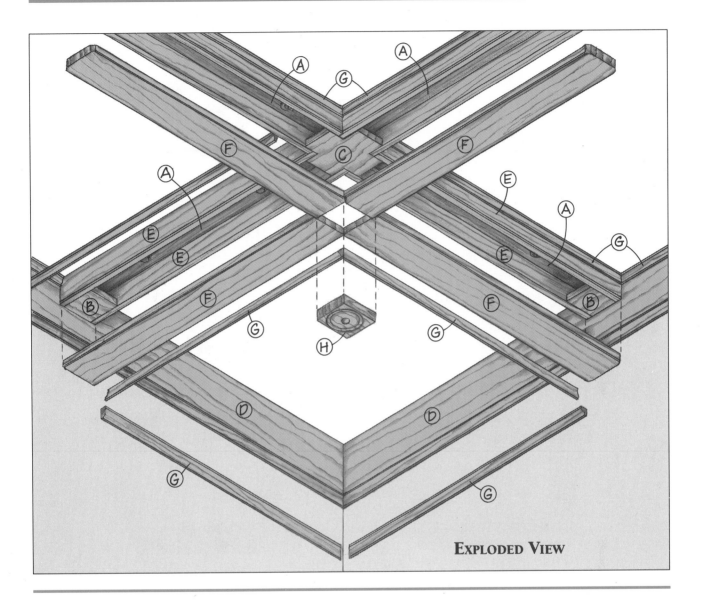

EXPLODED VIEW

MATERIALS LIST (FINISHED DIMENSIONS)

Parts

A. Grounding $3/4'' \times 3^{1}/4'' \times$ (variable)

B. Cleats $3/4'' \times 3^{1}/4'' \times 3^{1}/4''$

C. Cross cleats $3/4'' \times 6'' \times 6''$

D. Flat moldings $3/4'' \times 5'' \times$ (variable)

E. Beam sides $3/4'' \times 3^{1}/4'' \times$ (variable)

F. Beam caps $3/4'' \times 4^{3}/4'' \times$ (variable)

G. Beam moldings $3/4'' \times$ (variable) $\times$ (variable)

H. Rosettes $1^{1}/4'' \times 3^{1}/4'' \times 3^{1}/4''$

Hardware

#10 x 2″ Roundhead wood screws
#10 Molly anchors
1/4″ x 2″ Lag screws
#8 x 1″ Flathead wood screws
#8 x 1½″ Flathead wood screws
1/4″ Flat washers
4d Finishing nails
6d Finishing nails

Note: The dimensions shown will make a beam 4¾ inches wide and 4 inches deep, a good size for rooms with a ceiling 8 to 10 feet high and 150 to 400 square feet of ceiling area. However, you may adjust the dimensions depending on the size of your room and the effect you want to achieve.

The amount of hardware needed will depend on the size of the room and the design of the coffering.

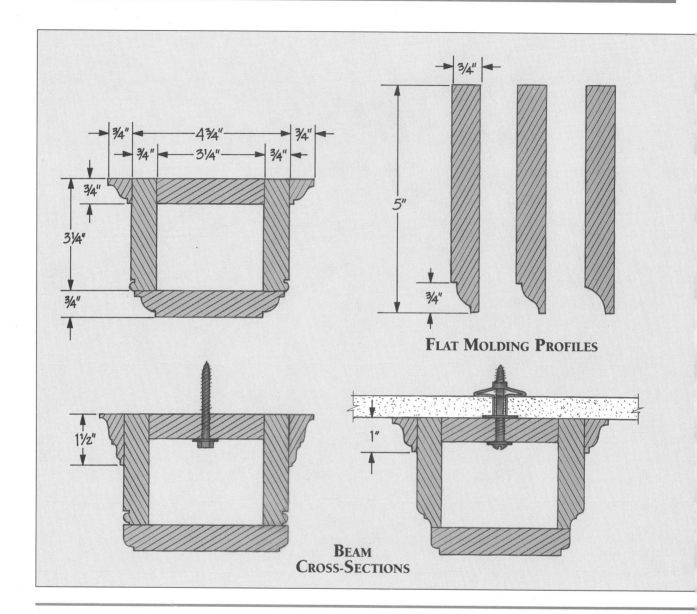

FLAT MOLDING PROFILES

BEAM CROSS-SECTIONS

PLAN OF PROCEDURE

1 Choose a design and calculate the materials required. While all coffered ceilings are built in a similar manner, there are many different designs that you might use. The *Beam Cross-Sections* and the *Flat Molding Profiles* show just a few possibilities. You can combine different molded shapes depending on your tastes and the effect you're after. If you're undecided, sketch cross-sections of beams until you hit upon a design that pleases you.

Carefully measure your ceiling and make a scale drawing. Decide how you want to apply the grid. How many beams will run parallel to the ceiling joists? How many will run perpendicular to them?

How big will the recesses be between the beams? Sketch the location of your beams on the drawing.

Note: In most coffered ceilings, the beams are spaced evenly, 40 to 60 inches apart, and the recesses are as nearly square as possible. Even a large room may require only 4 to 6 beams — 2 or 3 running parallel to the ceiling joists and 2 or 3 more running perpendicular.

2 Select and prepare the stock. Using your drawing, figure the materials you will need. Use an inexpensive utility wood for the grounding and cleats, scraps of ¾-inch plywood for the cross cleats, and

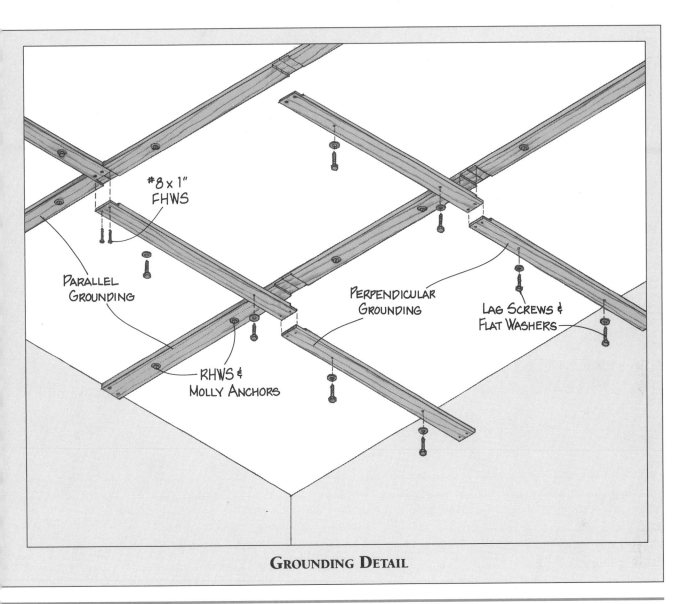

GROUNDING DETAIL

cabinet-grade lumber for the moldings and beam parts. On the coffered ceiling shown, the grounding and cleats are made from #2 pine, while the coffering is done in white oak, stained to match the oak trim in the rest of the house.

Plane the rosette stock to 1¼ inches thick, and the remaining stock to ¾ inch thick. Rip the lumber for the grounding, cleats, flat moldings, beam sides, and beam caps to width.

3   Install the grounding.   Measure the locations of the beams on the ceiling and snap chalk lines to indicate the centerline of each beam. Using a stud

finder, find the joists in the ceiling and mark their location and direction.

Put up the grounding that runs parallel to the joists first. Since it's not likely that the location of the grounding strips will coincide with the joists, use molly anchors and roundhead wood screws to fasten the grounding to the ceiling. (If you get lucky and can locate a strip of parallel grounding over a joist, secure it with lag screws.) Cut lap joints wherever the perpendicular grounding strips will cross the parallel grounding. If you need to splice two or more strips together, butt them end to end at the lap joints, as shown in the *Grounding Detail.*

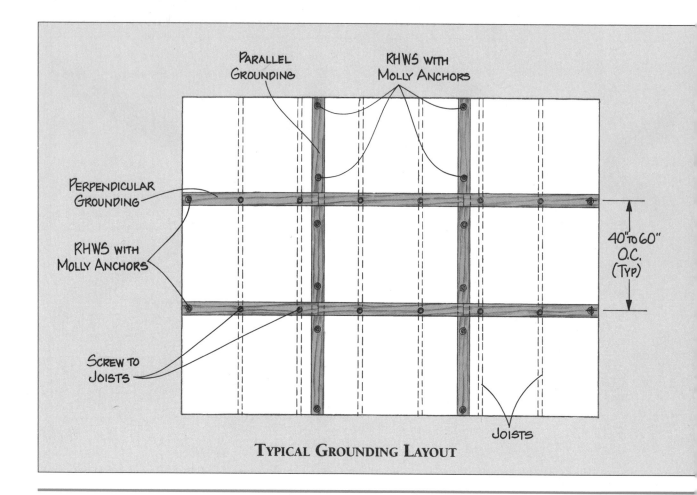

PARALLEL
GROUNDING

RHWS WITH
MOLLY ANCHORS

PERPENDICULAR
GROUNDING

RHWS WITH
MOLLY ANCHORS

SCREW TO
JOISTS

40" TO 60"
O.C.
(TYP)

JOISTS

TYPICAL GROUNDING LAYOUT

Apply the perpendicular grounding over the parallel strips. Once again, cut lap joints where the strips cross, and if you need to splice strips, do so at the lap joints. Fasten the perpendicular grounding to the ceiling with lag screws wherever the strips cross the joists. (*See Figure 7-1.*)

Secure the lap joints with #8 x 1-inch flathead wood screws. Fasten the ends of the grounding strips (where they meet the walls) with molly anchors and round-head wood screws. (*See Figure 7-2.*)

7-1 When installing the grounding, only the strips that run *perpendicular* to the joists can be attached directly to the framing. Most of the parallel strips will be fastened to the ceiling drywall. For this reason, apply the perpendicular grounding over the parallel grounding. When the perpendicular strips are fastened to the joists, they will help to hold up the parallel strips.

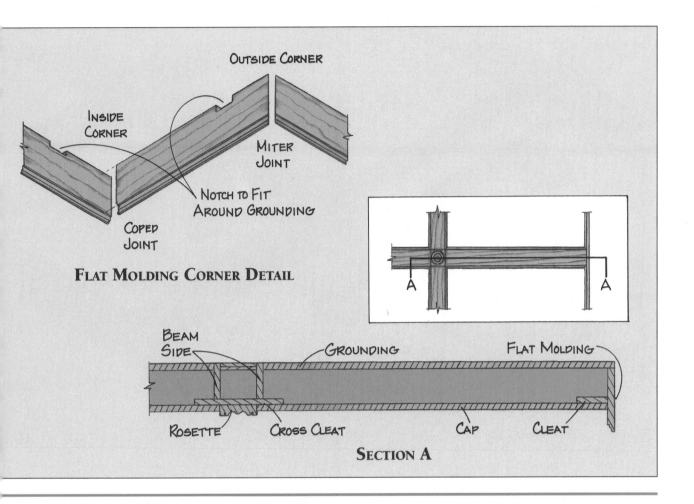

INSIDE CORNER

OUTSIDE CORNER

MITER JOINT

NOTCH TO FIT AROUND GROUNDING

COPED JOINT

FLAT MOLDING CORNER DETAIL

A ——— A

BEAM SIDE

GROUNDING

FLAT MOLDING

ROSETTE   CROSS CLEAT   CAP   CLEAT

SECTION A

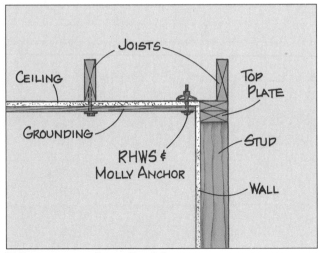

CEILING

JOISTS

TOP PLATE

GROUNDING

RHWS & MOLLY ANCHOR

STUD

WALL

7-2 To secure the ends of the grounding strips, fasten them to the ceiling with roundhead wood screws and molly anchors. Later, the face molding will also help to support the grounding strip ends.

4 Cut the shapes of the moldings.   Shape the lower edge of the flat moldings and beam sides with a router or shaper. (Remember, the flat area of the flat molding must be as wide or wider than the beams are tall. The shaped portion of the flat molding should stick out beneath the installed beams, as shown in *Section A.*) Also cut the shapes of the beam caps and beam moldings. Finish sand all the moldings.

A SAFETY REMINDER

If the beam moldings are narrower than 1 inch, shape the edge of a wider board, then rip the moldings free. Don't try to rout or shape narrow stock; it may splinter or kick back.

5 Temporarily install the flat moldings. Cut the flat moldings to length, mitering the outside corners and coping the inside corners. Notch the top

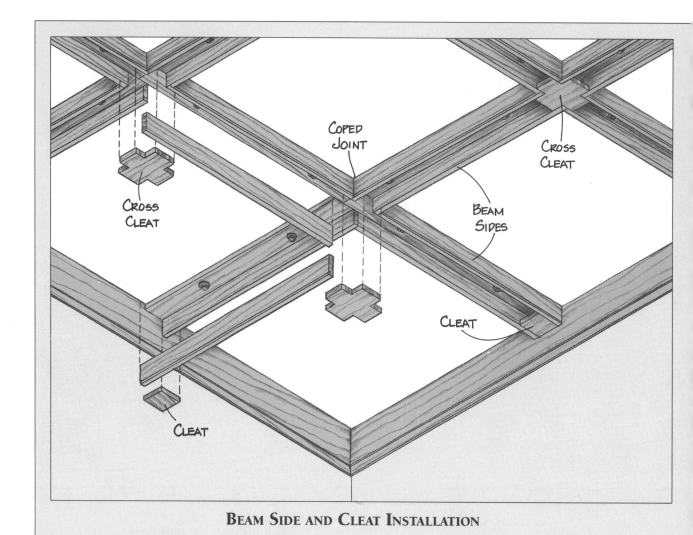

BEAM SIDE AND CLEAT INSTALLATION

edges of the boards to fit around the grounding, as shown in the *Flat Molding Corner Detail*. Tack it to the wall with 6d finishing nails, but don't drive the nails all the way home yet. (*See Figure 7-3.*)

FOR BEST RESULTS

If the ceiling isn't perfectly horizontal, scribe and cut the top edges of the flat moldings to fit the imperfections in the ceiling. The *lower* edge of the flat molding should be perfectly straight.

6   Temporarily install the beam sides.   Cut and fit the beam sides to the grounding, coping the corners, as shown in the *Beam Side and Cleat Installa-*

tion. (Because the beam sides frame the rectangular spaces created by the grounding, all the corners will be inside corners — so they all should be coped.) Temporarily fasten the beam sides to the grounding with #8 by $1^1/_2$-inch flathead wood screws. (*See Figure 7-4.*)

FOR BEST RESULTS

If the ceiling isn't flat, scribe the top edges of the beam sides and cut them to fit the ceiling, just as you did the flat moldings. The bottom edges of the beam sides should be straight across and relatively level.

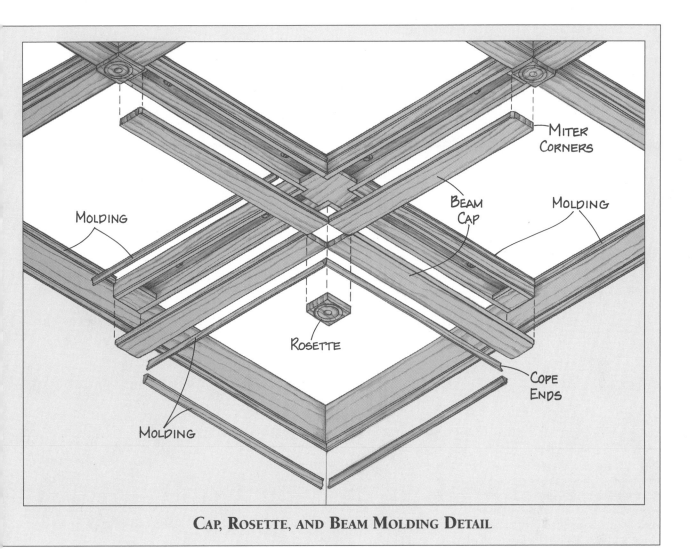

CAP, ROSETTE, AND BEAM MOLDING DETAIL

Labels on illustration: MITER CORNERS, BEAM CAP, MOLDING, MOLDING, ROSETTE, COPE ENDS, MOLDING, MOLDING

7-3 Fit the flat moldings to the walls, mitering the outside corners and coping the inside corners. Notch the top edges as needed to fit around the grounding. If you must splice two lengths of flat molding, join them with a scarf joint. Position the scarf joints under the grounding — most of the joint will be hidden when you install the beams. Tack the moldings in place temporarily. Leave the heads of the nails showing so you can easily remove the moldings and apply a finish.

7 **Finish and assemble the flat molding and the beam sides.** On simple trim projects, craftsmen usually fit *all* the parts, then finish them all at once before installing them permanently. However, because the fit of the caps, rosettes, and beam moldings depends on how the flat moldings and the beam sides lay when they're installed, it's best to finish these parts now and attach them permanently before proceeding.

Remove the beam sides and the flat moldings, carefully numbering the pieces so you can put them up again in the same locations. Apply a stain (if desired) and all but the last coat of finish. (*See Figure 7-5.*) When the finish cures, install the flat moldings and the beam sides permanently. Set the heads of the finish nails below the surface and cover them with wood putty, but don't apply the last coat of finish yet.

TRY THIS TRICK

Buy a neutral color of wood putty and mix it with the stain you used for the moldings. This will match the putty and the wood as closely as possible.

8 **Attach the cleats and cross cleats.** Wherever the beams butt against the flat moldings, you must install cleats, and wherever they cross, you must install cross cleats. These cleats keep the beam sides properly spaced and provide a surface to which the caps and the rosettes can be attached.

Count the number of cleats and cross cleats you need. Cut the cleats from utility lumber and the cross

7-4 Fit the beam sides to the grounding, coping the corners. Attach the beam sides temporarily with flathead wood screws, countersinking the heads flush with the wood surface. **Note:** The beam moldings will hide the screw heads on the completed coffering.

7-5 Remove the beam sides and the flat moldings and apply a finish. The parts of the coffering shown were stained with a water-soluble aniline dye because it soaks into the hard oak, creating a deeper and more permanent color than ordinary pigment stains. After the dye dried completely, the surface was finished with a mixture of tung oil and spar varnish (10 parts oil to 1 part varnish). This finish builds to a deep gloss after several coats, and it's very easy to repair should you accidentally scratch the moldings when reinstalling them.

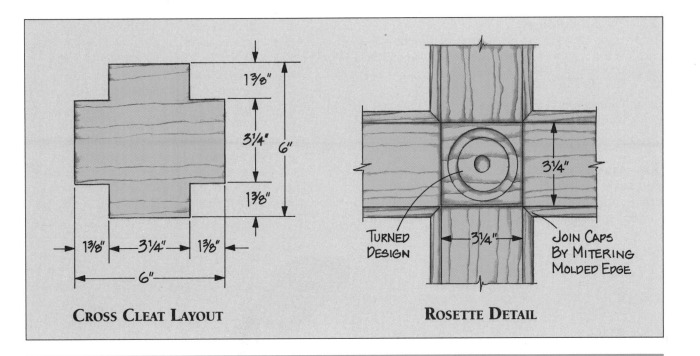

CROSS CLEAT LAYOUT

ROSETTE DETAIL

TURNED
DESIGN

3¼"

3¼"

JOIN CAPS
BY MITERING
MOLDED EDGE

1⅜"

3¼"

6"

1⅜"

1⅜"   3¼"   1⅜"

6"

---

cleats from scraps of plywood. Fasten both parts between the beam sides with 4d finishing nails. Set the nail heads and cover them with wood putty.

9   Turn the rosettes.   Create the rosettes on a drill press or lathe. You can purchase cutters for a drill press that will make rosettes, or you can turn them on a lathe with a faceplate attachment. (*See Figure 7-6.*)

10   Fit the caps and rosettes to the beams.   Fit the caps to the beams. Butt the ends of the caps to the

flat moldings; however, where the beams cross, miter the cap corners so the molded edges fit together, as shown in the *Rosette Detail*. Temporarily tack the caps in place.

Cut the rosettes to fit the spaces where the caps come together. These spaces won't be perfectly square, nor will they all be exactly the same size. You'll have to trim each rosette to fit a specific space. When it fits, mark the edges so you can put it back in exactly the same position.

7-6 Turn the rosettes on a lathe as faceplate turnings. Fasten each block to the faceplate with double-faced carpet tape. Cut a combination of beads and coves that works visually with the shapes you have chosen for the moldings.

11 Fit the moldings. Fit the beam moldings inside the recesses created by the beams, coping the corner joints, as shown in the *Cap, Rosette, and Beam Molding Detail*. (As with the beam sides, all corners will be inside, so all the joints will be coped.) Press the moldings into place to make sure they fit, but don't fasten them to the beams yet. Carefully mark the moldings so you know where to install each piece.

12 Finish and assemble the caps, rosettes, and beam moldings. Remove the caps from the beams, marking them so you can put them back in the same position. Stain these parts, if necessary, then apply all but the last coat of finish. Put the caps and the rosettes in place, attaching them with 4d finishing nails. (*SEE FIGURE 7-7.*) Set the heads of the nails and cover them with wood putty.

Apply the last coat of finish to the flat moldings and all the beam parts, including the beam moldings that you haven't yet installed. Let the finish dry completely, then secure the beam moldings to the beams with 4d finishing nails. (*SEE FIGURE 7-8.*) Once again, set the heads and cover them with putty. Touch up the finish around the nail heads and anywhere else you may have accidentally scratched it.

7-7 After staining and finishing the caps and rosettes, permanently attach them to the cleats and the beam sides with finishing nails. To prevent the nails from working loose, drive them at a slight angle. Alternate the angle with each nail, driving the first nail to the right, the next to the left, and so on.

7-8 Completely finish the beam moldings before you install them so all you have to do is touch up the finish around the nail heads. This is much easier than trying to apply a stain upside down, and it helps prevent you from accidentally splashing finish on the walls or ceiling.

8

FOLDING POWER TOOL STAND

When working on site, one of the most common problems is finding a place to set up your power tools. Many craftsmen build makeshift workbenches by stretching a few planks between sawhorses. However, this solution creates another problem — you have to break down the workbench whenever you need to move the power tools or use the sawhorses.

This folding stand offers a better solution. It folds flat to store in a small space, but will support most miter saws and other benchtop tools when set up. Whether it's folded or set up, it can be easily wheeled from place to place. You can even use it as a dolly to help move heavy power tools.

This stand offers other advantages, too. There are two supports that pull out from the ends to help feed long boards. You can use one stand for several different tools, changing quickly from tool to tool. You can even make a router table to attach to the stand, enabling you to shape moldings and trim on the job.

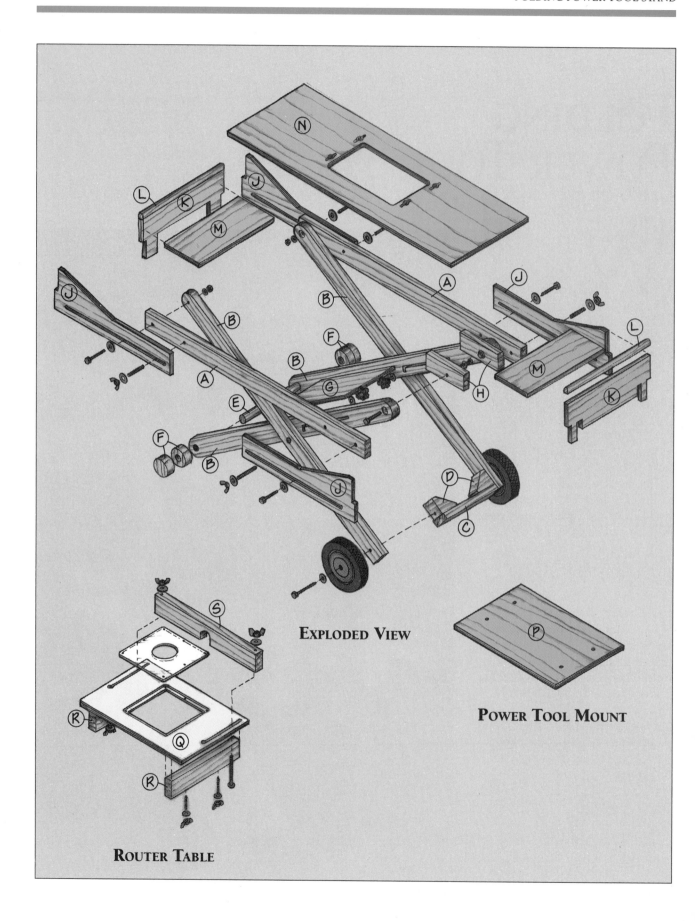

EXPLODED VIEW

POWER TOOL MOUNT

ROUTER TABLE

MATERIALS LIST (FINISHED DIMENSIONS)

Parts

A. Stretchers
(2)   1¼" x 3⅛" x 46½"
B. Legs (4)   1¼" x 3⅛" x 53"
C. Wheel
spacer   1¼" x 3⅛" x 11"
D. Wheel
blocks (2)   2½" x 3¼" x 3¼"
E. Handle   1¼" dia. x 13½"
F. Feet (4)   3⅛" dia. x 1¼"
G. Stiffener   ¾" x 8½" x 20"
H. Handle leg
mounts (2)   1¼" x 3⅛" x 8"
J. Support
sides* (4)   ¾" x 7½" x 24"
K. Support
ends* (2)   ¾" x 7½" x 17½"
L. Support edges†
(2)   ¾" x (variable) x 17½"
M. Support
stiffeners* (2) ¾" x 7¾" x 16"
N. Top*   ¾" x 16" x 46½"
P. Power tool
mount*   ¾" x (variable) x
(variable)

Q. Router table‡   ¾" x 14" x 21"
R. Router table supports
(2)   1¼" x (variable) x 14"
S. Router table
fence   1¼" x 3⅛" x 21"

*Make these parts from plywood.
†Make these parts from hardwood.
‡Make this part from laminate-covered particleboard.

Hardware

Stand
#8 x 1½" Flathead wood screws
(48)
#8 x 3" Flathead wood screws (18)
½" x 4" Lag screws (2)
⅜" x 2" Lag screws (2)
⅜" x 3½" Hex bolts (2)
⅜" x 3¼" Hex bolts (2)
⅜" x 3" Hex bolts (2)
⅜" x 3" Hanger bolts (4)
½" Flat washers (4)
⅜" Flat washers (4)

⅜" x 1½" Fender washers (10)
⅜" Stop nuts (4)
⅜" Wing nuts (4)
⅜" Star knobs (2)
8" x 1¾" Lawn mower wheels
with bearings (2)

Power Tool Mount

5/16" x 3" Hanger bolts (4)
¼" Flat washers (4)
5/16" Wing nuts (4)

Router Table

#8 x 1½" Flathead wood screws
(4)
#8 x ¾" Flathead wood screws (8)
⅜" x 5" Carriage bolts (2)
5/16" x 3" Hanger bolts (4)
⅜" x 1¼" Fender washers (2)
¼" Flat washers (4)
⅜" Wing nuts (2)
5/16" Wing nuts (4)
⅜" x 9¼" x 9¼" Clear acrylic
plastic

PLAN OF PROCEDURE

1 Select the stock and cut the parts to size.
To make the folding power tool stand, you need five 8-foot-long two-by-fours (as straight and as clear as you can find), 1 sheet of ¾-inch cabinet-grade plywood, a scrap of hardwood, and a 14-inch-long piece of closet pole. If you wish to make the optional router table, you'll need a 2-foot-square piece of particleboard or medium-density fiberboard (MDF). (You can substitute a laminated sink cutout for the particleboard.)

Calculate the variable dimensions in the Materials List. To do this, determine which power tool you will use most often on this stand (probably your miter saw). Measure the size of the base and the height of the worktable above the base. The length and width of the power tool mount must be 1 to 2 inches larger than the base. Figure the width of the support edges so they will be even with the worktable when the tool is fastened to the stand. (Remember to allow ¾ inch for the thickness of the power tool mount.) Figure the width of the router table supports so the table surface will be even with the support edges.

Cut the legs and stretchers to length. Joint one face and one edge of each two-by-four part to eliminate any warp or twist. Plane the two-by-four parts to 1¼ inches thick and rip them to 3⅛ inches wide. Glue two short lengths of two-by-four together to make the thick stock needed for the wheel blocks. Then cut all the parts to size. If necessary, apply laminate to the top surface of the router table.

FOR BEST RESULTS

Whether you use a laminated sink cutout or decide to laminate the top of the router table yourself, apply several coats of tung oil to the *uncovered* surface as soon as possible. Otherwise, it will absorb and release moisture more readily than the laminate-covered surface, causing the router table to warp.

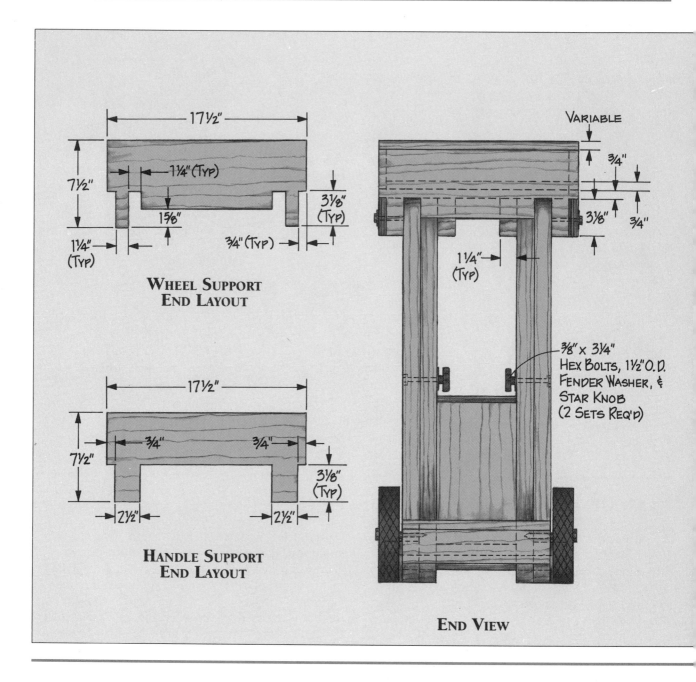

**WHEEL SUPPORT
END LAYOUT**

**HANDLE SUPPORT
END LAYOUT**

END VIEW

2 Drill the holes in the stand parts. Lay out the locations of the holes and slots in the stretchers, legs, feet, support sides, top, handle leg mounts, and power tool mount. Then drill these holes:

■ 1¼-inch-diameter holes through the handle legs and two of the feet to fit the handle, as shown in the *Handle Leg Assembly/Side View*

■ 1-inch-diameter holes in the top to mark the corners of the cutout, as shown in the *Top Layout*

■ ⅞-inch-diameter holes in the top to fasten the power tool mount

■ ⅜-inch-diameter holes with 1-inch-diameter, ⅜-inch-deep counterbores in the handle legs for the pivot bolts

■ ⅜-inch-diameter holes with 9/16-inch-diameter, ⅜-inch-deep counterbores in the wheel legs for the locking bolts, as shown on the *Wheel Leg Assembly/Side View*

■ ⅜-inch-diameter holes in the wheel leg for the pivot bolts

■ ⅜-inch diameter holes in the stretchers for the wheel leg pivot bolts, as shown in the *Stretcher Layout*

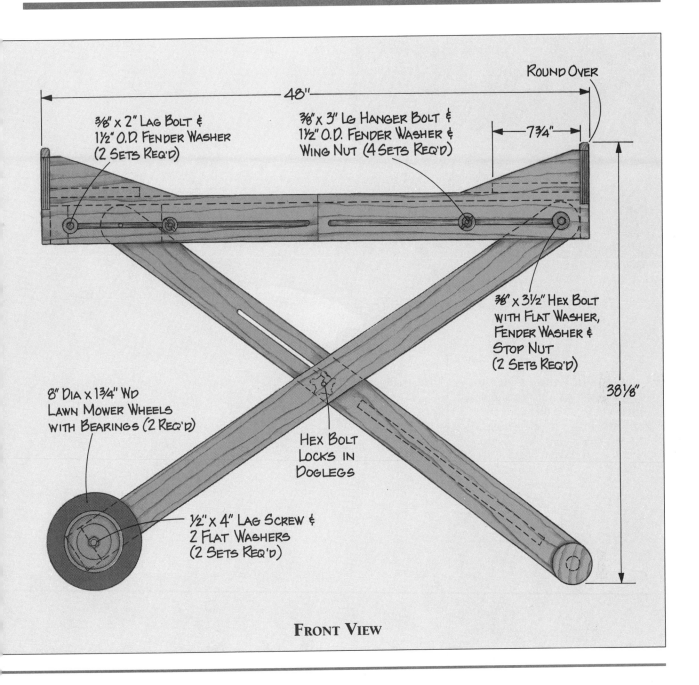

ROUND OVER

48"

3/8" x 2" LAG BOLT &
1½" O.D. FENDER WASHER
(2 SETS REQ'D)

3/8" x 3" LG HANGER BOLT &
1½" O.D. FENDER WASHER &
WING NUT (4 SETS REQ'D)

7¾"

3/8" x 3½" HEX BOLT
WITH FLAT WASHER,
FENDER WASHER &
STOP NUT
(2 SETS REQ'D)

38⅛"

8" DIA x 1¾" WD
LAWN MOWER WHEELS
WITH BEARINGS (2 REQ'D)

HEX BOLT
LOCKS IN
DOGLEGS

½" x 4" LAG SCREW &
2 FLAT WASHERS
(2 SETS REQ'D)

FRONT VIEW

■ 3/8-inch diameter holes in the handle leg mounts for the handle leg pivot bolts, as shown in the *Handle Leg Mount Layout*

■ 3/8-inch-diameter holes in the top, support sides, and handle legs to mark the ends of the slots

■ 5/16-inch-diameter pilot holes in the stretchers for the lag screws and hanger bolts that hold the support assemblies to the stand

■ 1/4-inch-diameter pilot holes in the power tool mount for the hanger bolts, as shown in the *Power Tool Mount Layout*

3 **Rout the slots in the stand parts.** Using a portable router and a straight bit, rout the 3/8-inch-wide slots in the top, the support sides, and the handle legs. (SEE FIGURES 8-1 AND 8-2.) Note that each handle leg slot has a 3/4-inch dogleg at one end, as shown in the *Handle Leg Assembly/Side View*. To make this dogleg, cut each slot as if it were two separate slots. Rout the long portion first, then the short one.

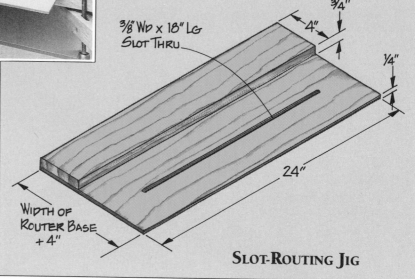

8-1 **To rout the 3/8-inch-wide slots** in the stand parts, make this simple jig. Glue a long, straight board (the *straightedge*) to a piece of 1/4-inch plywood (the *base*), as shown, and clamp the jig to a scrap board. Using a straight bit, rout a 3/8-inch-wide, 18-inch-long slot through the base.

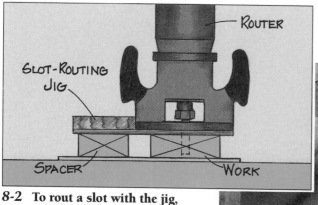

8-2 **To rout a slot with the jig,** clamp the part to the workbench or hold it fast with double-faced carpet tape. (If the part isn't wide enough to support the jig, secure scraps to the workbench around the part. These scraps must be the same thickness as the part.) Place the jig over a part, aligning the sides of the slot in the base with the layout lines on the part. Clamp the jig in place and rout the slot.

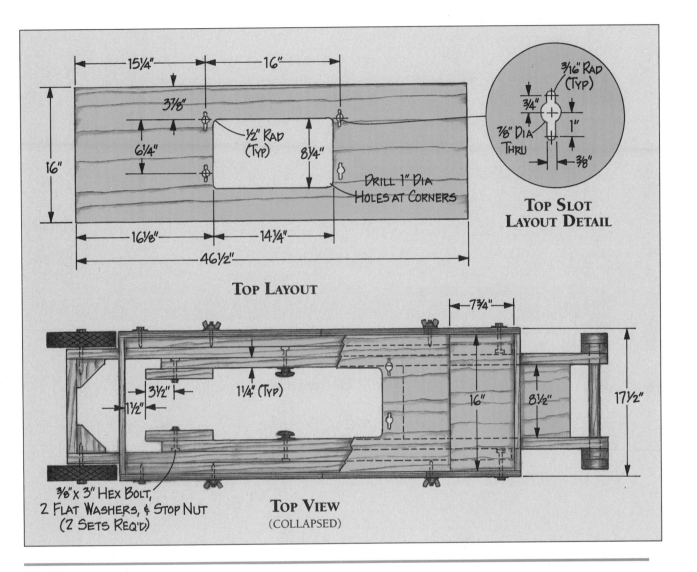

TOP LAYOUT

TOP SLOT LAYOUT DETAIL

TOP VIEW (COLLAPSED)

⅜" x 3" HEX BOLT, 2 FLAT WASHERS, & STOP NUT (2 SETS REQ'D)

4 Cut the shape of the stand parts. Lay out the shapes of:
- The support sides, as shown in the *Support Side Layout*
- The wheel support end, as shown in the *Wheel Support End Layout*
- The handle support end, as shown in the *Handle Support End Layout*
- The handle legs and feet, as shown in the *Handle Leg Assembly/Side View*
- The wheel blocks, as shown in the *Wheel Leg Assembly/Top View*
- The wheel legs, as shown in the *Wheel Leg Assembly/Side View*

Cut the shapes with a band saw or saber saw. Also make the cutout in the top, as shown in the *Top Layout*. Sand the sawed edges.

5 Build the handle leg and wheel leg assemblies. To make the handle leg assembly, glue together the handle legs, handle, and feet. Let the glue dry, then fasten the stiffener between the handle legs with glue and #8 x 3-inch flathead wood screws. Attach the handle leg mounts to the legs with ⅜-inch x 3-inch hex bolts, flat washers, and stop nuts. Tighten the stop nuts so they're snug, but not so tight that the legs won't pivot easily.

To make the wheel leg assembly, fasten together the wheel legs, wheel spacer, and wheel blocks with glue and #8 x 3-inch flathead wood screws. Drill ⅜-inch-diameter, 3-inch-deep pilot holes through the legs and the blocks to mount the wheels, as shown in the *Wheel Leg Assembly/Side View*.

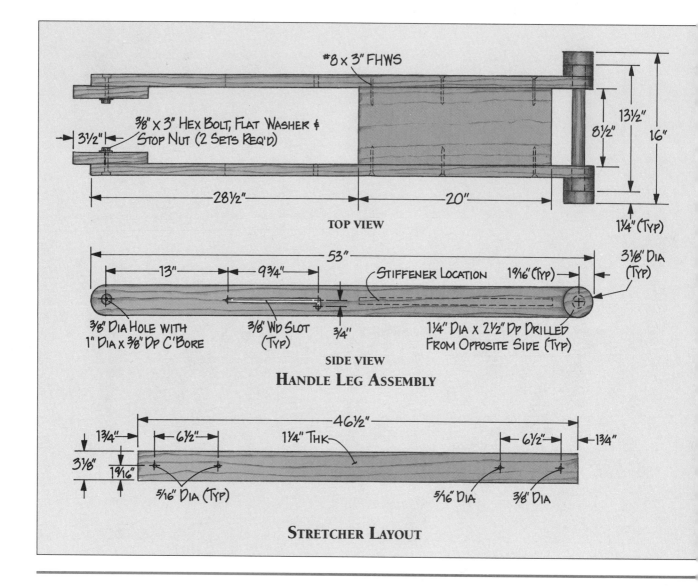

TOP VIEW

SIDE VIEW
HANDLE LEG ASSEMBLY

STRETCHER LAYOUT

6 Assemble the stand. Attach the wheel leg assembly to the handle leg assembly with 3/8-inch x 3¼-inch hex bolts, fender washers, and star knobs. Fold the wheel assemblies flat and place them between the stretchers. Temporarily secure the wheel legs to the stretchers by inserting 3/8-inch x 3½-inch hex bolts through the pivot holes. Fasten the top to the stretchers with glue and #8 x 1½-inch flathead wood screws.

Position the handle leg mounts as shown in the *Top View,* and fasten them to the top with #8 x 3-inch flathead wood screws. Secure the lawn mower wheels to the wheel legs with ½-inch x 4-inch lag screws and flat washers. Tighten the lag screws until they're snug, but not so tight that the wheels won't turn.

7 Attach the supports. With the legs still folded, remove the wheel leg pivot bolts and position the support sides on the stretchers. Fasten the support sides to the stretchers with lag screws, hanger bolts, fender washers, and wing nuts, as shown in the *Front View.* Put fender washers on the pivot bolts, then insert the bolts through the support sides, stretchers, and wheel legs. Secure the support sides, stretchers, and wheel legs with flat washers and stop nuts.

Tighten the lag screws and the stop nuts on the pivot bolts so the fender washers are snug against the support sides, but without preventing the supports from sliding back and forth easily. To lock the supports in place, tighten the wing nuts on the hanger bolts.

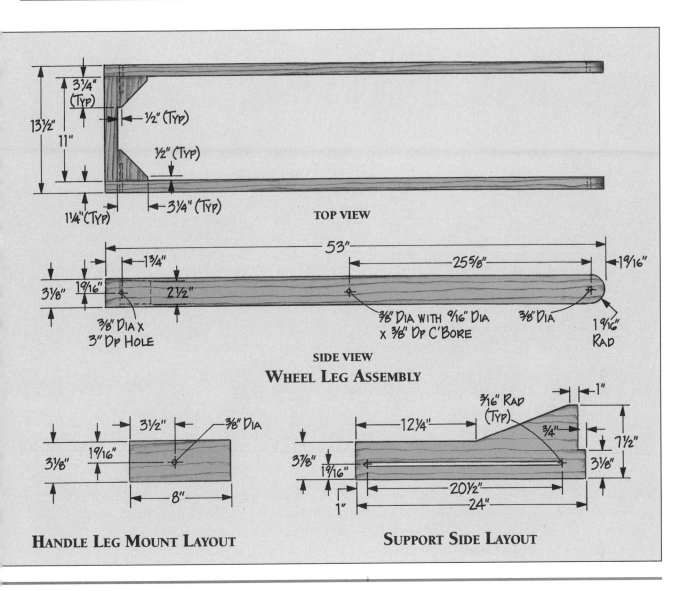

TOP VIEW

3¼" (TYP)
13½"
11"
½" (TYP)
½" (TYP)
1¼" (TYP)
3¼" (TYP)

SIDE VIEW
WHEEL LEG ASSEMBLY

53"
1¾"
25⅝"
1 9/16"
3⅛"
1 9/16"
2½"
⅜" DIA x
3" DP HOLE
⅜" DIA WITH 9/16" DIA
x ⅜" DP C'BORE
⅜" DIA
1 9/16"
RAD

HANDLE LEG MOUNT LAYOUT

3½"
⅜" DIA
1 9/16"
3⅛"
8"

SUPPORT SIDE LAYOUT

3/16" RAD
(TYP)
1"
12¼"
¾"
7½"
3⅛"
3⅛"
1 9/16"
1"
20½"
24"

Attach the support ends and support stiffeners to the supports with glue and #8 x 1½-inch flathead wood screws. Round over the top surfaces of the support edges and glue them to the support ends.

8 Prepare the power tool mount. Drill holes in the power tool mount so you can bolt or screw the base of the power tool to it. Drive 5/16-inch x 3-inch hanger bolts into the underside of the mount until the screw threads are completely engaged. Part of the hanger bolts will protrude from the top of the mount. Mark the bolts flush with the top surface, back them out, and cut them off with a hacksaw. Then drive the hanger bolts back into the power tool mount. Fasten flat washers and wing nuts on the bottom ends of the bolts.

9 Drill the holes in the router table parts. If you elect to make the router table attachment, drill these holes in the parts:

■ 7/8-inch-diameter holes through the table, as shown in the *Router Table/Top View*

■ ⅜-inch-diameter holes in the fence for the mounting bolts, as shown in the *Router Table/Front View*

■ ⅜-inch-diameter holes to mark the ends of the slots in the router table

■ ¼-inch-diameter pilot holes in the router table supports for the hanger bolts, as shown in the *Router Table/End View*

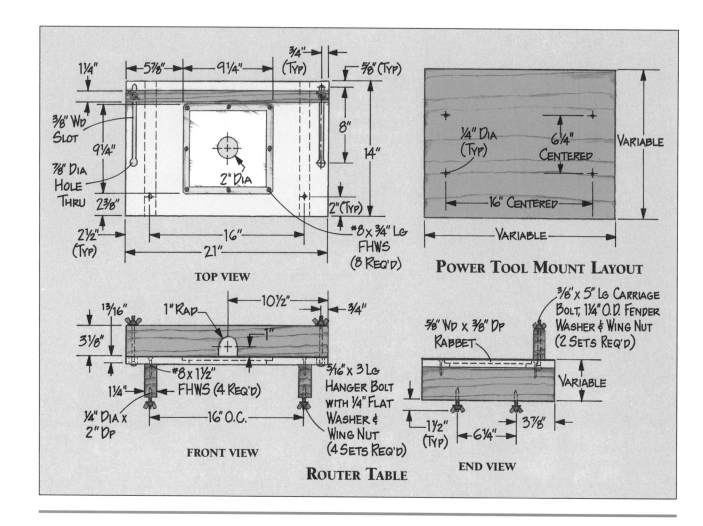

TOP VIEW

POWER TOOL MOUNT LAYOUT

FRONT VIEW

ROUTER TABLE

END VIEW

10 **Rout the slots in the table.** With a router and a straight bit, cut the ³⁄₈-inch-wide slots in the router table. Use the slot-routing jig to guide the router, as shown in *FIGURES 8-1 AND 8-2* on page 100.

11 **Make the cutout and rabbet for the mounting plate.** The mounting plate must be inset in the router table, flush with the top surface. To do this, first cut the rabbets that the mounting plate will rest in, then remove the waste from inside the rabbets. (*SEE FIGURES 8-3 THROUGH 8-5.*)

12 **Make the cutout in the fence.** Lay out the cutout in the fence, as shown in the *Router Table/Front View*. Make this cutout with a band saw or a saber saw, then sand the sawed edges smooth.

13 **Assemble the router table.** Fasten the router table to the router table supports with #8 x 1¹⁄₂-inch flathead wood screws. Drive ⁵⁄₁₆-inch x 3-inch hanger

bolts into the bottom edges of the supports, and fasten flat washers and wing nuts on the bottom ends. Insert ³⁄₈-inch x 5-inch carriage bolts through the fence, and secure the fence to the table with wing nuts and fender washers.

14 **Finish the stand, power tool mount, and router table.** Remove the hardware from the stand, breaking it down into several small assemblies — the wheel leg assembly, handle leg assembly, support assemblies, and top assembly. Also remove the hardware from the power tool mount and the router table. Set the hardware aside.

Mix 4 parts tung oil and 1 part spar varnish — this makes a tough but easy-to-apply finish. Wipe on several coats with a rag, covering all the wooden surfaces of the assemblies and parts. Let the finish dry completely, then rub it out with paste wax and buff thoroughly. Reassemble the stand, power tool mount, and router table.

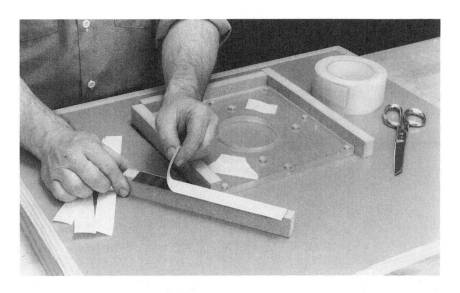

8-3 To install the mounting plate in the router table, first tack the plate to the table with small pieces of double-faced carpet tape. Stick 1-inch thick blocks all around the plate, forming a frame. The inside dimensions of this frame must be the same as the outside dimensions of the plate. Remove the plate from inside the frame.

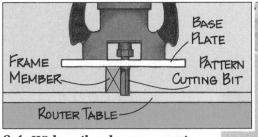

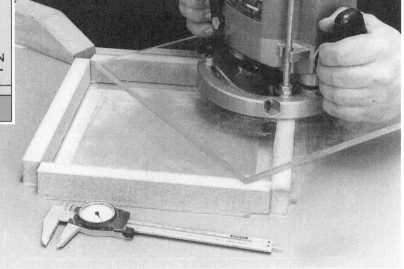

8-4 With a piloted pattern-cutting bit, rout the rabbet that will hold the mounting plate in the router table. Use the frame that you stuck to the table to guide the bit, and check the work with a caliper as you go — the rabbet must be the same depth as the plate is thick. To help balance the router on the frame, use the mounting plate as an oversize base.

8-5 After routing the rabbet in the worktable, cut out the waste with a saber saw. Drill a hole in the waste, insert the blade of the saw through the hole, and cut along the inside edges of the rabbet. After removing the waste, clean up the sawed edges with a file. Round the corners of the mounting plate to match the corners of the rabbets and secure the plate in the router table with #8 x $^{3}/_{4}$-inch flathead wood screws.

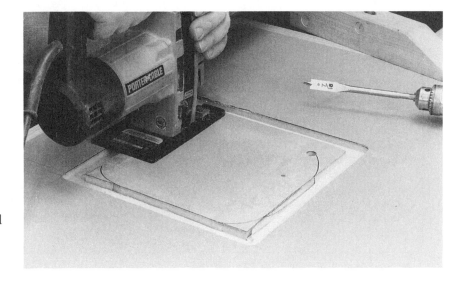

USING THE FOLDING POWER TOOL STAND

This stand is specifically designed to support miter saws, router tables, and the kinds of bench-top power tools that you would commonly use in finish carpentry. It will support an enormous amount of weight — many times that of a miter saw — but an extremely heavy tool will make the stand top heavy. For safety, don't mount a tool heavier than 75 pounds.

1 **To use the stand, turn it on** its side. Loosen the star knobs that lock the legs together and pull on the ends of the legs. They will fold out from underneath the top. Seat the locking bolts in the doglegs — the short segments of the slots in the handle legs. Tighten the star knobs and lift up the top, setting the stand on its legs. To fold the stand flat, reverse this process.

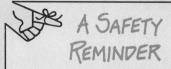

A SAFETY REMINDER

Always rest the stand on its side when folding the legs in or out. Because the stand folds like a giant scissors, you could hurt yourself badly if you attempt to fold the stand when it's standing on its feet. The stand may drop down and pinch your hands or fingers.

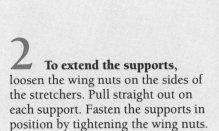

2 **To extend the supports,** loosen the wing nuts on the sides of the stretchers. Pull straight out on each support. Fasten the supports in position by tightening the wing nuts.

3 **To mount a power tool on** the stand, fasten the base of the tool to the power tool mount. (If you wish to mount more than one power tool, make several mounts.) Align the wings on the wing nuts with the slots in the top of the stand. Lower the power tool mount so the wing nuts, washers, and hanger bolts fit through the slots and the $^{7}/_{8}$-inch-diameter holes in the top. Slide the mount forward in the slots and tighten the wing nuts. **Note:** The router table attaches to the stand in the same manner.

9

STAINED-GLASS AND CUT-GLASS WINDOWS

As a homeowner, you may dream of adding an elegant stained-glass or cut-glass window to your home. Perhaps you've run across an attractive window at an antique store or an artist's studio and thought about how it might look in a special nook. But how would you install it? Could you make it as energy efficient as the other windows in your home?

Install a stained-glass or cut-glass window just like any other. First, install the glass in a sash and construct a case around it. Prepare a rough opening, then fasten the case in the opening. To reduce thermal loss, add a second sash glazed with clear insulating glass outside the stained or cut-glass sash.

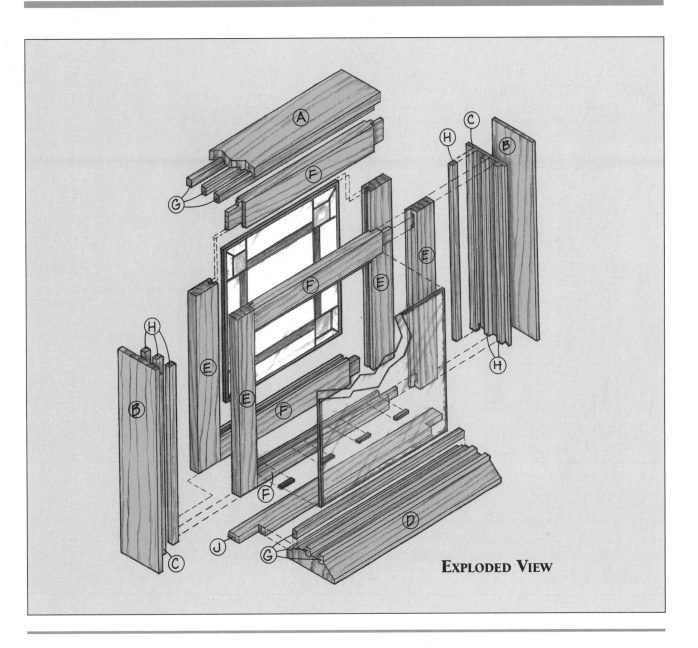

EXPLODED VIEW

MATERIALS LIST (FINISHED DIMENSIONS)

Parts

A. Head
jamb   3/4″ x 4⁹/₁₆″* x (variable)

B. Side jambs
(2)   3/8″ x 4⁹/₁₆″* x (variable)

C. Side jamb overlays
(2)   3/8″ x 4⁹/₁₆″* x (variable)

D. Sill   1½″ x 5⁹/₁₆″* x (variable)

E. Sash stiles
(4)   1″ x 2½″ x (variable)

F. Sash rails
(4)   1″ x 2½″ x (variable)

G. Head/sill
stops (6)   ½″ x 3/4″ x (variable)

H. Side
stops (6)   ½″ x 3/4″ x (variable)

J. Stool   3/4″ x (variable) x
(optional)   (variable)

*Use these dimensions for homes with
drywall-covered walls. Add 3/4″ for
homes with plaster-and-lath walls.*

Hardware

#8 x 1½″ Flathead wood screws
Stained glass or cut glass
Insulating glass
Large glazing points
Rubber gasket (to make setting
blocks)
Glazing compound
Silicone caulk

Note: *The amount of hardware needed
will depend on the size of the window.*

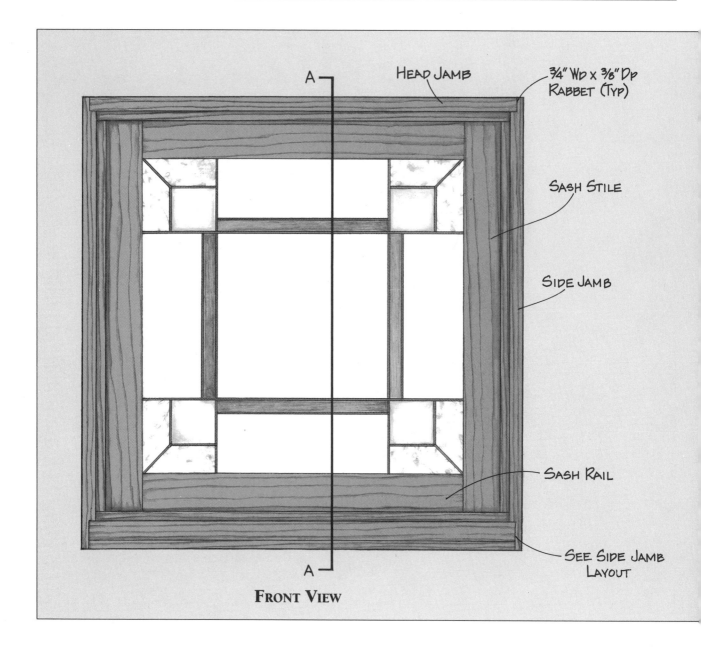

FRONT VIEW

PLAN OF PROCEDURE

1 Figure the dimensions of the parts. Measure the height and width of the stained glass or cut glass. Use these dimensions to figure the length of the sash and case members. First calculate the overall size of the sash. They must be 4 inches taller and 4 inches wider than the glass. Then figure the length of the individual members:

■ The length of the sash stiles equals the glass height plus 4 inches.

■ The length of the sash rails equals the glass width plus 3 inches.

Once you know the size of the sash, you can calculate the size of the case that will enclose them. It must be 2¼ inches taller and 1½ inches wider than the sash. Also figure the length of the members:

■ The length of the side jambs equals the sash height plus 2¼ inches.

■ The length of the side jamb overlays equals the sash height plus ¾ inch.

■ The length of the head jamb and sill equals the sash width plus ¾ inch.

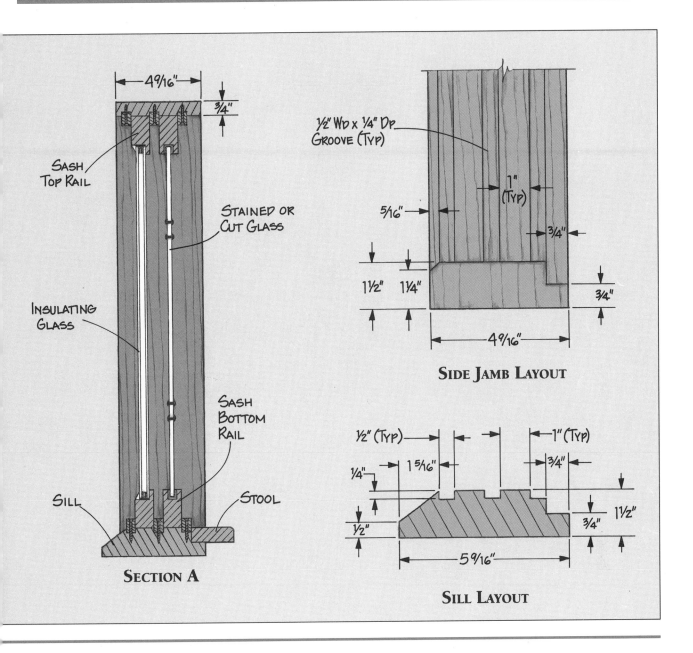

SECTION A

SIDE JAMB LAYOUT

SILL LAYOUT

The length of the stops depends on the inside dimensions of the case — it's best to figure these *after* the case is assembled.

The stool is optional. Whether you need a stool depends on how you will trim the window, and the size of the stool depends on the design of the trim.

2 Select the stock and cut the parts to size. Purchase clear cabinet-grade lumber to make the sash and case parts. Cut the case members and sash members to the sizes you have figured. Rip the stops to the proper thickness and width, but don't cut them to length yet.

3 Cut the rabbets and grooves in the sash members. The members of the inside sash are grooved to hold the stained glass or cut glass, as shown in *Section A*. Measure the thickness of the glass. If it's ½ inch or less, cut ½-inch-wide, ½-inch-deep grooves in the inside sash members. If it's thicker, adjust the width of the groove to accommodate the glass.

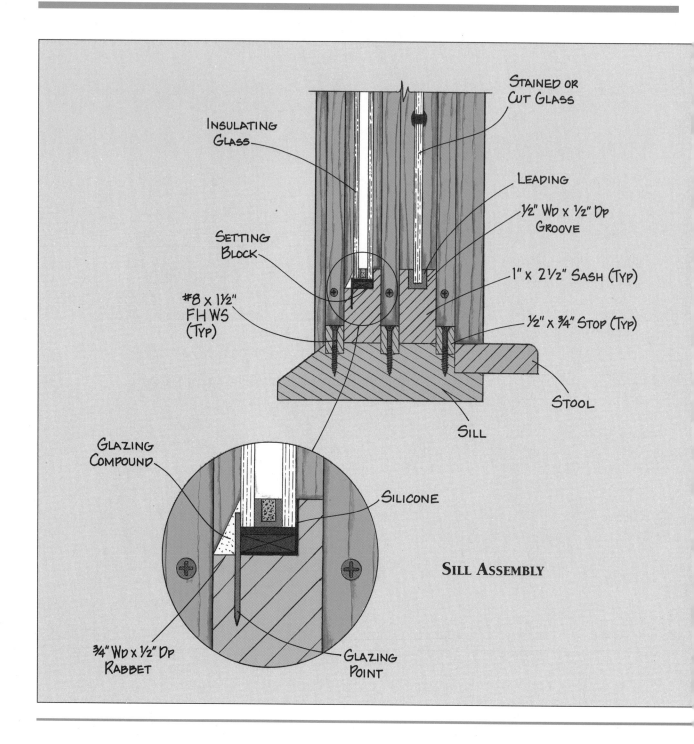

INSULATING GLASS

STAINED OR CUT GLASS

LEADING

½" WD x ½" DP GROOVE

SETTING BLOCK

1" x 2½" SASH (TYP)

#8 x 1½" FHWS (TYP)

½" x ¾" STOP (TYP)

STOOL

SILL

GLAZING COMPOUND

SILICONE

SILL ASSEMBLY

¾" WD x ½" DP RABBET

GLAZING POINT

The members of the outside sash are rabbeted to hold the insulating glass. Cut ³/₄-inch-wide, ½-inch-deep rabbets in the edges of the outside sash members, as shown in the *Sill Assembly* drawing.

4 Cut the mortises and tenons in the sash members. Both the inside and outside sash are joined with mortises and tenons. Make ½-inch-wide,

1½-inch-long, 1⁹/₁₆-inch-deep mortises near the ends of the sash stiles, as shown in the *Outside Sash Joinery Detail* and *Inside Sash Joinery Detail*. **Note:** If you've cut grooves wider than ½ inch in the inside sash members, make the mortises the same width as the grooves.

Fit the tenons to the mortises. Cut 2-inch-long tenons on the ends of the inside sash rails, then cut

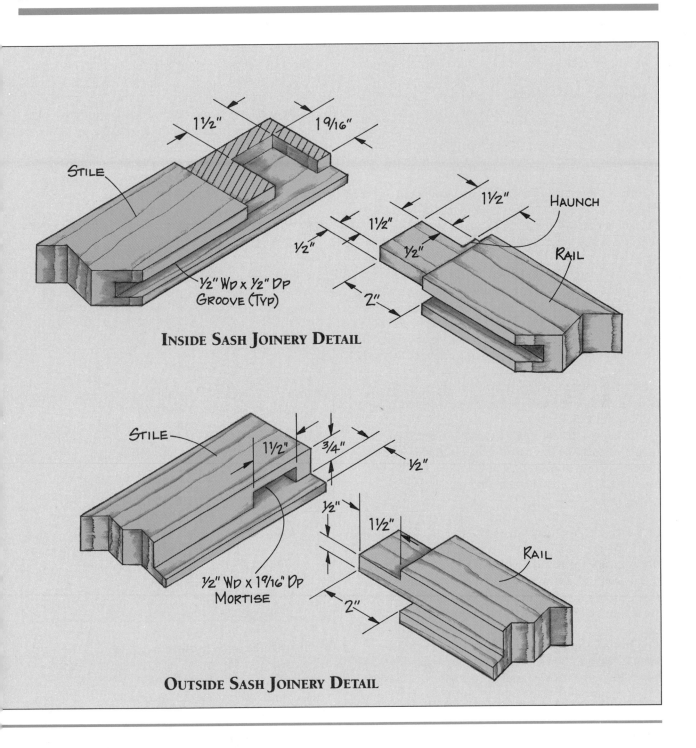

INSIDE SASH JOINERY DETAIL

Stile — 1½" — 1⁹/₁₆" — ½" Wᴅ x ½" Dᴘ Groove (Tʏᴘ) — ½" — 1½" — ½" — 2" — Haunch — Rail

OUTSIDE SASH JOINERY DETAIL

Stile — 1½" — ¾" — ½" — ½" — 1½" — 2" — ½" Wᴅ x 1⁹/₁₆" Dᴘ Mortise — Rail

a 1½-inch-wide, ½-inch-deep notch in the outside edge of each tenon, creating a *haunch*. (This haunch will fill the groove in the stile when the mortise-and-tenon joint is assembled.) Cut the tenons on the outside rails, making the cheeks different lengths. The cheeks on the *inside* surfaces should be 2 inches long, while those on the outside surfaces are 1½ inches long.

Temporarily dry assemble (without glue) the sash to

check the fit of the joints. Leave them assembled until you can fit the sash to the case.

5 Cut the grooves in the case members. The head jamb, sill, and side jamb overlays are all grooved to hold the stops. Cut ½-inch-wide, ¼-inch-deep grooves in these members, spacing them as shown in the *Side Jamb Layout*.

6 Cut the shape of the side jamb overlays.

The bottom ends of the side jamb overlays are coped to fit the upper surface of the sill. Stack the two overlays together, inside face to inside face, and fasten them with double-faced carpet tape. Lay out the shape of the sill on the outside surface of one overlay, then cut the shape in both parts with a band saw, saber saw, or coping saw. Take the stack apart and discard the tape.

7 Assemble and finish the case and sash.

Finish sand the case members. Attach the overlays to the side jambs with waterproof glue. Then assemble the side jambs, head jamb, and sill with glue and flathead wood screws. Clamp or brace the assembly so it's perfectly square while the glue dries.

Test fit the sash in the assembled case. There should be a 1/32- to 1/16-inch-wide gap between the sash and the case all the way around the perimeter of the assemblies. (This will let the sash members expand.) If the fit is too tight, plane the outside edges of the sash until they fit properly.

Cut the stops to length and secure them in the grooves in the case with flathead wood screws. Do *not* glue them in the grooves.

Disassemble the sash members and finish sand them. Reassemble the outside sash with glue. Do any necessary touch-up sanding and apply a finish to the assembled case, outside sash, and members of the inside sash.

Reassemble the inside sash, but *don't* glue the members together. You may need to take them apart someday to repair the stained glass or cut glass. Instead, dry assemble them and slide the glass into the grooves. If the glass isn't as thick as the grooves are wide, insert small wooden wedges in the grooves on the *outside* surface to keep it from shifting in the sash.

8 Install the insulating glass in the outside

sash. Have a glass shop make up an insulating pane about 1/4 inch narrower and 3/8 inch shorter than the inside dimensions of the rabbets in the outside sash. If the glass shop offers rubber *setting blocks* for sale, purchase enough to mount the window. If not, buy a thick rubber gasket (available in the plumbing department of most hardware stores), and cut 1/2-inch-wide, 3/4-inch-long blocks from it.

Fill the rabbet with clear silicone caulk. Place the setting blocks on the bottom ledge of the rabbet, pressing them into the silicone and spacing them every 6 to 8 inches. (Extended contact with moisture will deteriorate the seal around insulating glass. Setting blocks keep the bottom edge of the insulating

glass above any moisture that might find its way into the rabbet.) Set the bottom edge of the window on the blocks, then swing it into the sash and press it against the silicone.

Let the silicone set up, then peel off any excess that has squeezed out from under the pane. As an added precaution, secure the pane in the sash with glazing points, spacing them every 8 to 12 inches around the perimeter of the pane. Seal the pane in the sash with glazing compound.

FOR YOUR INFORMATION

Insulating glass is made up of two panes of ordinary 1/8-inch-thick glass spaced about 1/4 inch apart by an aluminum channel. The channel is *desiccated;* that is, it holds chemicals that absorb moisture. The space between the glass is filled with an inert gas, usually argon. The desiccants and the nonreactive gas keep the inside surfaces of the glass panes perfectly clean and clear. The outside edge of the insulating glass is secured with a sealant and a rubber gasket. When installing this pane, you must be careful of this gasket. Don't nick it or cut it. If you break the seal, opening the space between the panes to the outside air, the window will begin to cloud over.

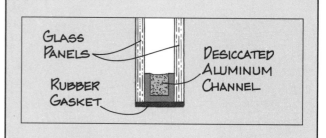

9 Install the sash in the case.

Remove the inside and outside stops from the case. (Leave the middle stops in place.) Rest the assembled sash against the middle stop and replace the inside and outside stops to secure them. Caulk the seams around the outside stops to weatherproof the window.

10 Install the window.

Remove the inside stops and take the inside sash out of the case before you install it in your home. Set the stained-glass or cut-glass sash in a safe place where it won't get broken while you make a rough opening and secure the case. (Refer to "Installing Windows" on page 40 for instructions on how to install the case.) After the case is fastened in the wall, replace the inside sash.

10

PANELED DOOR

Are you restoring an older home and need to replace several doors? Or do you have an odd-size door opening and can't find a commercial unit to fit it? Or do you want to give a room a touch of class with special doors and trim made from rich hardwoods? If you can answer yes to any of these questions, consider making your own paneled doors.

A paneled door is a simple project that you can make with ordinary woodworking tools. It's a standard frame-and-panel construction — the rails and stiles are joined by mortises and tenons; the panels rest in grooves in the inside edges. Often, the inside edges are shaped or there is a decorative molding around the perimeter of the panels.

PLAN OF PROCEDURE

1 Decide on a door design. There are many ways to put a frame-and-panel door together. *FIGURE 10-1* shows four common designs. Most doors have five structural parts — two *door stiles*, a *head rail*, a *lock rail*, and a *kick rail*. (The "ladder" design simply has a head rail and a kick rail with several *intermediate rails* in between.) There also may be short vertical frame members called *mullions*, which further divide the door. The rectangular spaces between the stiles, rails, and mullions are filled with wooden *panels* or, in some cases, glass panes or *glazing*.

2 Calculate the size of the door. Door sizes vary widely. Generally, they are 24 to 36 inches wide and 78 to 90 inches tall. To figure the size of the door you need, measure the rough opening. Subtract $2\frac{1}{2}$ inches from both the width and the height — this will allow the proper amount of room for both the door and the jambs. If there is a door jamb already installed in the opening, measure the jamb opening and subtract $\frac{1}{8}$ inch from the width and $\frac{5}{8}$ inch from the height.

3 Figure the dimensions of the door parts. Make a rough sketch of the door and list the parts — stiles, rails, mullions, and so on. Figure the thickness, width, and length of each part. (*SEE FIGURE 10-2.*) These dimensions depend not only on the door's design and size, but also on its joinery. For example, the head, lock, and kick rails are usually joined to the stiles with through mortise-and-tenon joints. This will make them longer than intermediate rails, which are held in the grooves with stub tenons. (See the *Rail-to-Stile Joinery Detail* and the *Intermediate Rail and Mullion Joinery Detail.*) The door's intended use also plays a part in the dimensions. Exterior doors are usually thicker than interior doors.

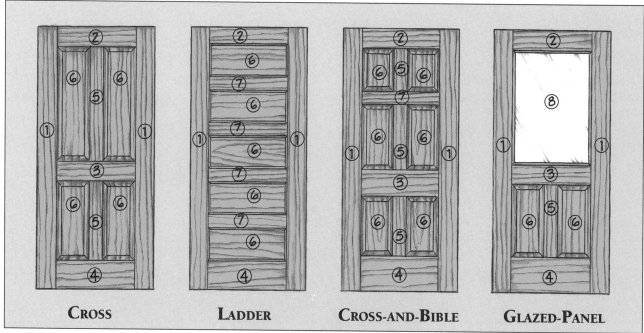

CROSS   **LADDER**   **CROSS-AND-BIBLE**   **GLAZED-PANEL**

10-1 There are many ways to design and construct a paneled door, but they all have some parts in common. The standard *cross* door consists of two *stiles* (1), a *head rail* (2), a *lock rail* (3), and a *kick rail* (4). The short vertical frame members are *mullions* (5). The rectangular spaces in the frame are filled with floating wooden *panels* (6). The *ladder* door is similar, but it has no lock rail or mullions. Instead, there are several *intermediate rails* (7) between the head rail and the kick rail. In the *cross-and-bible* door, the frame defining the four upper panels is said to represent a cross, while the two lower panels are an open Bible. It uses all the above-mentioned parts — stiles, head rail, lock rail, kick rail, intermediate rail, and mullions. You can also make a *glazed-panel* door for exterior use by substituting *insulating glass* (8) for one or more of the wooden panels.

4 **Select the stock and cut the parts to size.**
Once you've determined the size of the parts, figure how much lumber you'll need. To build a 1¼-inch-thick door frame, purchase 6/4 (six-quarters) cabinet-grade lumber. For thicker doors, purchase 8/4 (eight-quarters) lumber. Purchase 4/4 (four-quarters) or 6/4 stock for the panels.

Don't plane the lumber yet. Instead, bring it back to your shop and let it rest for three or four weeks to "shop dry" — that is, let it reach equilibrium with the relative humidity in the shop. If you work the wood too soon, it will likely be in motion (expanding or contracting) while you're trying to fit the parts together.

Rough out the frame parts — cut them about 2 inches longer and 1 inch wider than needed. Joint one face and an adjacent edge of each part, making sure the two surfaces are perfectly flat and square to one another. Plane the other face to thickness and rip the other edge to width. Then cut the boards to length. This will make the rails, stiles, and mullions as straight and as true as possible.

Plane the lumber for the panels and panel molding to the required thickness. Glue boards edge to edge to make the wide stock for the panels and cut them to length. Allow room for the panels to expand and contract in the grooves. Set the molding stock aside — don't cut it yet.

10-2 **Interior doors are usually** 1¼ to 1½ inches thick; exterior doors are 1½ to 1¾ inches thick. The widths of rails, stiles, and mullions vary from 4 to 14 inches, depending on the door design and where they're used in the door. The lengths of the parts depend on the size of the door and how the parts are joined.

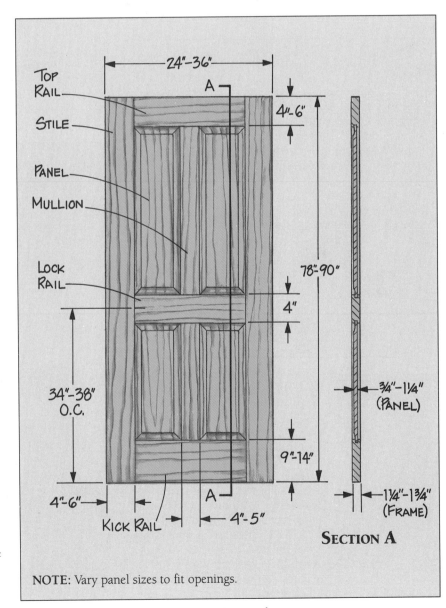

NOTE: Vary panel sizes to fit openings.

5 Cut grooves in the edges of the frame parts.
The inside edges of all the frame parts — rails, stiles, and mullions — are grooved to hold the panels. Cut the grooves with a router or a dado cutter. If you intend to install insulating glass in one or more frame openings, cut the grooves even though you won't use them. The grooves simplify the joinery, and later you can fill the portions of the grooves you don't need with wooden strips.

6 Cut the mortises in the stiles. Cut through mortises in the stiles where you will join the head, lock, and kick rails. To make each mortise, drill a line of overlapping holes in the stile to remove most of the waste. Then clean up the sides of the mortise and square the corners with a chisel. (SEE FIGURE 10-3.)

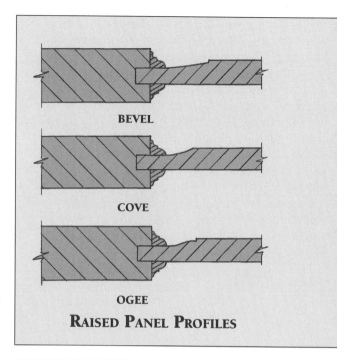

RAISED PANEL PROFILES

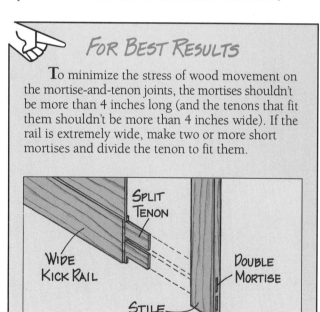

FOR BEST RESULTS

To minimize the stress of wood movement on the mortise-and-tenon joints, the mortises shouldn't be more than 4 inches long (and the tenons that fit them shouldn't be more than 4 inches wide). If the rail is extremely wide, make two or more short mortises and divide the tenon to fit them.

10-3 To make a mortise without a mortiser, first drill a row of overlapping holes to remove most of the waste. The diameter of the holes must equal the width of the groove in the stile. Then clean up the sides of the mortise with a chisel. To keep the sides flat and square to the edge, lay the stile on its side and clamp a spacer to the bench in front of it. (This spacer must be the same width as the tongues on each side of the groove.) Lay the back of the chisel on the spacer to guide the tool as you pare away the waste.

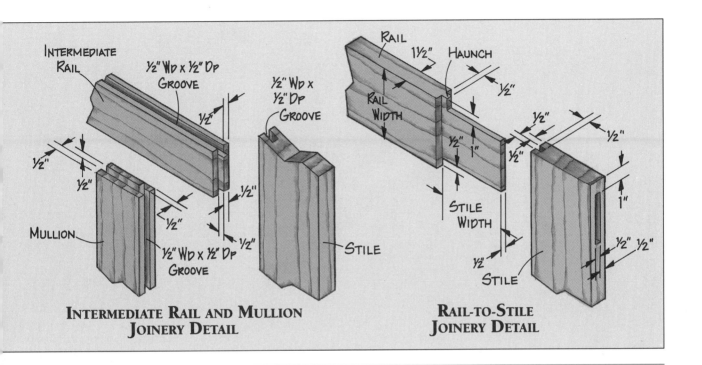

INTERMEDIATE RAIL
½" WD X ½" DP GROOVE
½" WD X ½" DP GROOVE
½"
½"
½"
½"
MULLION
½" WD X ½" DP GROOVE
½"
½"
GROOVE
STILE

INTERMEDIATE RAIL AND MULLION JOINERY DETAIL

RAIL
1½" HAUNCH
½"
RAIL WIDTH
½"
1"
½"
½"
½"
STILE WIDTH
1"
½"
½"
½"
STILE

RAIL-TO-STILE JOINERY DETAIL

7 Cut the tenons on the rails and mullions.
Using a table-mounted router or a dado cutter, cut the tenons on the ends of the rails and mullions. The tenons on the ends of the head, lock, and kick rails must fit the mortises in the stiles. Additionally, the tenons on the ends of the head and kick rails must be *haunched* to fit the grooved edges of the stiles. Notch the outside edges of the tenons to create the haunches, as shown in the *Rail-to-Stile Joinery Detail* and *Figure 10-4*.

As previously described, the intermediate rails and the mullions require only stub tenons. These must fit the grooves in the edges of the adjoining parts, as shown in the *Intermediate Rail and Mullion Joinery Detail*.

8 Raise the panels. For visual interest, you may cut *raised panels* to fill the frame — thick panels with tapered or thinned-out edges to fit the grooves. Cut these edges on a table saw, or use a table-mounted router and a panel-raising bit. (*See Figures 10-5 and 10-6.*) You can make a straight bevel with a saw blade or create coves, ogees, and other shapes with router bits, as shown in the *Raised Panel Profiles* drawing.

10-4 The tenons on the ends of the *outside* rails — the head and the kick rail — must be *haunched* to fill the grooved edges of the stiles. To make the haunch, notch the outside edge of the tenon.

10-5 To cut a raised panel on a table saw, tilt the blade 5 to 10 degrees. Attach a tall extension to the rip fence to help hold the face of the panel vertical while you cut it.

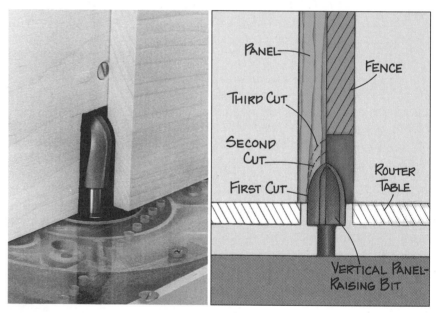

10-6 If you cut a raised panel on a router table, use a *vertical* panel-raising bit. (These are much safer than large-diameter wing cutters.) Cut the shape in several passes, extending the bit as needed to lengthen the thinned-out portion of the *tongue* around the perimeter of the panel.

9 Assemble the door. Finish sand the parts you have made so far — stiles, rails, mullions, and panels. Apply finish to the panels. Assemble the rails, stiles, and mullions with glue. (Use a waterproof glue if you're making an exterior door.) As you put the frame parts together, slide the wooden panels in place. However, *don't* glue the panels in the assembly; let them "float" in the grooves, free to expand and contract.

10 Make and install the molding. If you have elected to trim the perimeter of the panels, cut the profile of the panel molding into the edges of the stock

you set aside. Then rip the molding from the stock. If the door has raised panels with beveled edges, rip the molding at the same angle that you used to cut the bevels. (SEE FIGURE 10-7.)

Fit the molding to the inside edges of the frame, mitering the corners. (The molding will be too small to cope.) Finish sand the molding and fasten it in place with brads, as shown in the *Panel and Molding Joinery Detail*. Don't attempt to glue the molding to the frame and the panels — this will prevent the panels from expanding and contracting.

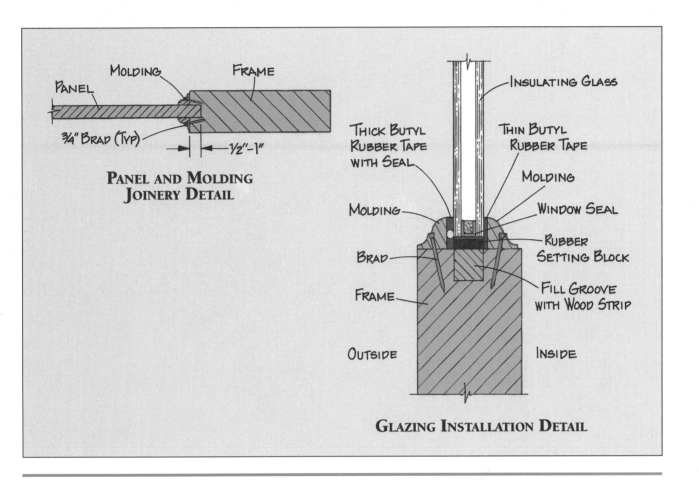

PANEL

MOLDING

FRAME

¾" BRAD (TYP)

½"–1"

**PANEL AND MOLDING
JOINERY DETAIL**

INSULATING GLASS

THICK BUTYL
RUBBER TAPE
WITH SEAL

THIN BUTYL
RUBBER TAPE

MOLDING

MOLDING

WINDOW SEAL

BRAD

RUBBER
SETTING BLOCK

FRAME

FILL GROOVE
WITH WOOD STRIP

OUTSIDE

INSIDE

GLAZING INSTALLATION DETAIL

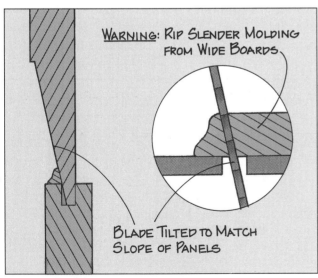

WARNING: RIP SLENDER MOLDING
FROM WIDE BOARDS

BLADE TILTED TO MATCH
SLOPE OF PANELS

10-7 If you have cut straight bevels
on the raised panels, you must also
bevel the adjoining face of the panel
molding, as shown. Rip the molding
with the blade tilted at the same angle
you used to make the raised panels.

VARIATIONS

If you have a shaper and plan to make several
doors, you may want to invest in a set of *stile-and-
rail cutters*. These matched cutters make *coped*
frame joints, eliminating the need for panel molding. Cut the grooves *and* shape the inside edges of
the frame parts in one operation. Then make the
tenons on the ends of the rails and mullions *and*
cope the shoulders to fit the shaped edges.

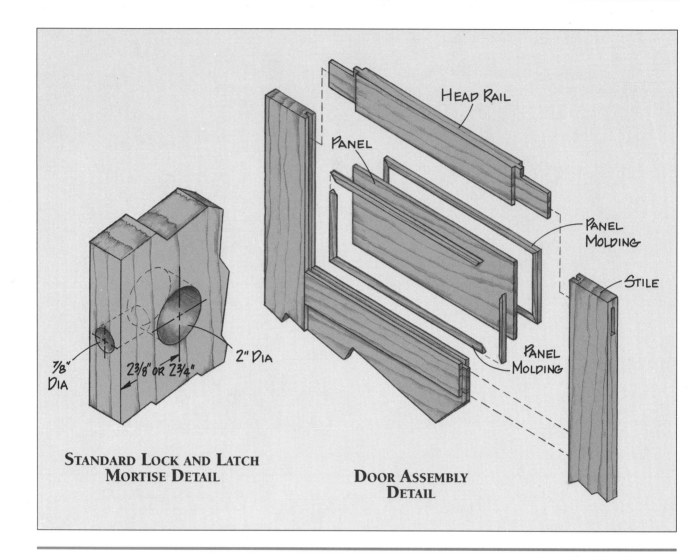

STANDARD LOCK AND LATCH MORTISE DETAIL

DOOR ASSEMBLY DETAIL

11 **Create a ledge to install glass.** If you plan to install insulating glass in the door frame, you must create a ledge on which the glass will rest. You can do this with the same molding you used to trim the panels. First, fill the grooves in the inside edges of the frame opening with wood strips, as shown in the *Glazing Installation Detail*. Fit *two* sets of molding to the opening and attach one to the door frame with waterproof glue and brads, near the *inside* (private side) of the door.

12 **Finish and hang the door.** Cut the hinge mortises in the hinge stile and drill the mortises for the lock and latch in the lock stile, as shown in the *Standard Lock and Latch Mortise Detail*. Do any necessary touch-up sanding, then apply a finish to the door. (Be sure to use a UV-resistant finish for an exterior door.)

If you plan to install glass, also finish the molding you haven't yet installed. Have a glass shop make up

an insulating pane the size you need. Also purchase from them rubber *setting blocks* and *butyl rubber tape*, both a thin tape and a thicker one with an integral seal. Line the surface of the ledge (the installed molding) with the thin tape. Place the rubber setting blocks on the *bottom* edge in the panel opening, spacing them approximately every 6 inches. Put the glass in place, resting it on the setting blocks. Cut strips of the thick rubber tape and lay them in place around the perimeter of the glass, on the outside surface. Install the outside molding with brads so it presses firmly against the tape and the glass. **Note:** You can substitute silicone caulk for the rubber tape, if you wish.

Hang the door as described in "Hanging a Door" on page 32. Finally, install the latch, lock, and strike plate.

INDEX

Note: Page references in *italic* indicate photographs or illustrations.
Boldface references indicate charts or tables.

WOODWORKING GLOSSARY

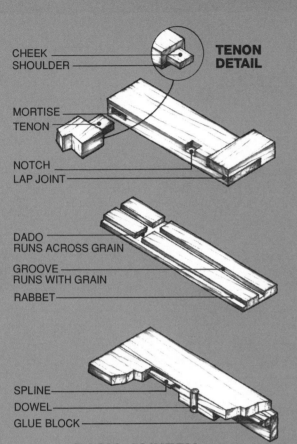

TENON DETAIL

CHEEK
SHOULDER

MORTISE
TENON

NOTCH
LAP JOINT

DADO
RUNS ACROSS GRAIN

GROOVE
RUNS WITH GRAIN

RABBET

SPLINE
DOWEL
GLUE BLOCK

BASIC JOINERY

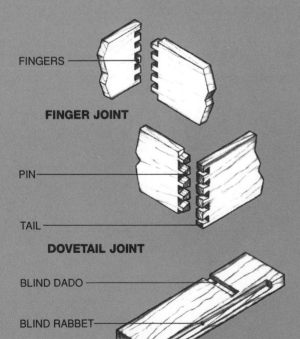

FINGERS

FINGER JOINT

PIN

TAIL

DOVETAIL JOINT

BLIND DADO

BLIND RABBET

SPECIAL JOINERY

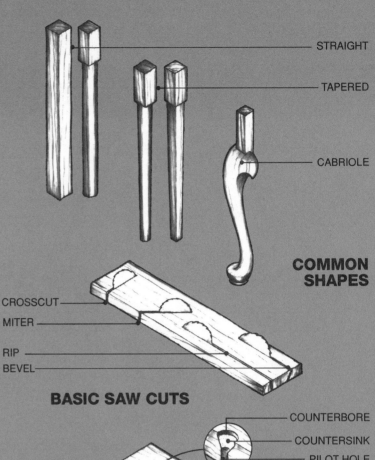

STRAIGHT

TAPERED

CABRIOLE

**COMMON
SHAPES**

CROSSCUT

MITER

RIP

BEVEL

BASIC SAW CUTS

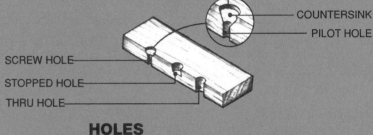

COUNTERBORE

COUNTERSINK

PILOT HOLE

SCREW HOLE

STOPPED HOLE

THRU HOLE

HOLES

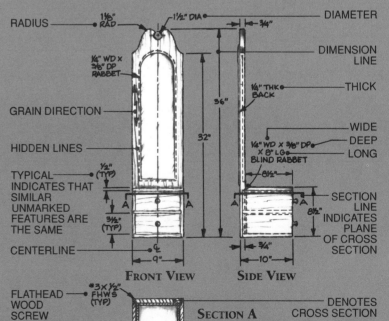

RADIUS — 1⅛" RAD

1½" DIA — DIAMETER

¾"

¼" WD × ⅜" DP RABBET

DIMENSION
LINE

⅛" THK
BACK — THICK

GRAIN DIRECTION

36"

32"

¼" WD × ⅜" DP
× 8" LG
BLIND RABBET

WIDE
DEEP
LONG

HIDDEN LINES

8½"

TYPICAL
INDICATES THAT
SIMILAR
UNMARKED
FEATURES ARE
THE SAME

½"
(TYP)

A   A

A   A

SECTION
LINE
INDICATES
PLANE
OF CROSS
SECTION

3½"
(TYP)

8½"

CENTERLINE

9"

¾"

10"

FRONT VIEW   **SIDE VIEW**

FLATHEAD
WOOD
SCREW

#3 × ½"
FHWS
(TYP)

SECTION A

DENOTES
CROSS SECTION

1/16" GAP BETWEEN
DRAWER & SIDE

ROUNDHEAD
WOOD SCREW

#3 × ½"
RHWS

SECTION A

PROJECT PLAN SYMBOLS